THE
PRACTICAL
STYLIST

THE PRACTICAL STYLIST

Fourth Edition

SHERIDAN BAKER

The University of Michigan

Thomas Y. Crowell
HARPER & ROW, PUBLISHERS
New York   Hagerstown   San Francisco   London

THE PRACTICAL STYLIST, Fourth Edition

Copyright © 1977, 1973, 1969, 1962 by Thomas Y. Crowell Company, Inc.

Library of Congress Cataloging in Publication Data

Baker, Sheridan Warner
  The practical stylist.

  1. English language — Rhetoric.   I. Title.
PE1408.B283   1977   808'.042   76-26601
ISBN 0-690-00873-2

Preface

This is a rhetoric and brief handbook primarily for freshman English, but it has also proved useful to others — advanced or struggling — who have found themselves facing a blank page and the problems of exposition. From the freshman's first essay through the senior's last paper (and on through the doctoral dissertation and the corporate annual report), the expository problems are always the same. Indeed, they all come down to two fundamental questions: one of form, one of style. And even form is spatial styling. Since, in general, writing well is writing in style, I have found it practical to teach writing almost as a tactile act, in which students learn how to shape their material and bring out the grain to best advantage. Hence *The Practical Stylist* — again revised extensively.

In this Fourth Edition, I have completely redone the exercises, seeking the most workable, both the proven and those newly evolved from teaching the text. I have improved Chapters One and Two with new examples, and with further clarification of the *pro*-and-*con* technique. A new chapter, Four, handles description and narration, which underlie much expository and argumentative writing; this chapter also discusses and illustrates the first and main function of exposition, describing a process, or more simply, giving directions. I have added "Definition" to the thoughts on "Evidence" in Chapter Five, and have moved the chapter on punctuation into the handbook, where it has seemed naturally to evolve. A new, more factual Research Paper illustrates how even straight exposition can take an argumentative edge to improve its thrust and organization. And again, I emphasize argument because I believe that argument subsumes all other expository principles and that it teaches clearly and easily the firmest organization of one's ideas. Throughout, in response to what teachers and students have told me, I have made hundreds of the quiet improvements that tell only in teaching. But in its content, its size, and its practical intent, *The Practical Stylist* remains essentially the same.

Many books on writing begin with simple units and build upward. I have found the opposite approach far more efficient —

beginning with the thesis, the big idea. Once students can push their material into an argumentative thesis and can grasp the large essentials of structural arrangement, they then can proceed easily to the smaller and more powerful elements—to paragraphs, to sentences, and on to the heart of the matter, to words, where the real dynamite of rhetoric is.

I have included exercises in thesis-making, in paragraphing, in writing various kinds of sentences and punctuating them, in using words and spelling them, and in handling various figures of speech. I have tried to encourage the student to play with language, to write unusual and complicated sentences for exercise, to juggle with words. The chapter on the research paper then draws these points together, bringing the student's expository skills fully to bear. The book concludes with a handbook of grammar, punctuation, spelling, capitalization, and usage—for supplementary and permanent reference—with further exercises as needed. Inside the front cover is a "do's" list against which the student may check his work; inside the back cover, a set of symbols for marking errors. Especially if the teacher likes to concentrate on students' writing in weekly essays arising from the exercises, the book serves well alone, or in company with *Problems in Exposition for The Practical Stylist* and with the expository readings of *The Essayist,* Third Edition, both designed to reinforce this book.

The teacher will find plenty of room here for any convenient approach, and ample opportunity for that almost necessary bonus of academic gratification, disagreeing with the book, out of which much of our best teaching comes. A great deal will certainly be familiar. Nothing here is really new; I am simply describing the natural linguistic facts discovered again and again by the heirs of Aristotle, in which lineage I seem inescapably to belong. For I have found that the one practical need in all writing is to mediate gracefully between opposite possibilities—between simplicity and complexity, clarity and shade, economy and plenitude, the particular and the general. I hope this book will help student and teacher to shoot the wickets pleasantly and well.

I wish to acknowledge my great debt to the teachers who, from the testing of some thirty-five thousand classrooms, have given me their encouragement and their suggestions. I am no less grateful to the many individual students and private citizens who have written me from as far away as Kenya and as near home as Ann Arbor.

SHERIDAN BAKER

Contents

One
Thesis

THE STYLISTIC APPROACH

Style in writing is something like style in a car, a gown, a Greek temple—the ordinary materials of this world so poised and perfected as to stand out from the landscape and compel a second look, something that hangs in the reader's mind, like a vision. It is your own voice, with the hems and haws chipped out, speaking the common language uncommonly well. It calls for a craftsman who has discovered the knots and potentials in his material, one who has learned to like words as some people like polished wood or stones, one who has learned to enjoy phrasing and syntax, and the very punctuation that keeps them straight. It is a labor of love, and like love it can bring pleasure and satisfaction.

Style is not for the gifted only. Quite the contrary. Everyone, indeed, already has a style, and a personality, and can develop both. The stylistic side of writing is, in fact, the only side that can be analyzed and learned. The stylistic approach is the practical approach: you learn some things to do and not to do, as you would learn strokes in tennis. Your ultimate game is up to you, but you can at least begin in good form. Naturally, it takes practice. You have to keep at it. Like the doctor and the lawyer and the golfer and the tennis player, you just keep practicing—even to write a practically perfect letter. But if you like the game, you can probably learn to play it well. You will at least be able to write a respectable sentence, and to express your thoughts clearly, without puffing and flailing.

In the essay, as in business, trying to get started and getting off on the wrong foot account for most of our lost motion. So you will start by learning how to find a thesis, which will virtually organize your essay for you. Next you will study the relatively simple structure of the essay, and the structure of the paragraph—the architecture of spatial styling. Then, for exercise, you will experiment with various styles of sentence, playing with length and complexity. And finally you will get down to words themselves. Here is where writing tells; and here, as in ancient times, you will be in touch with the mystery. But again, there are things to do and things not to do, and these can be learned. So, to begin.

WHERE ESSAYS FAIL

You can usually blame a bad essay on a bad beginning. If your essay falls apart, it probably has no primary idea to hold it together. "What's the big idea?" we used to ask. The phrase will serve as a reminder that you must find the "big idea" behind your several smaller thoughts and musings before you start to write. In the beginning was the *logos,* says the Bible—the idea, the plan, caught in a flash as if in a single word. Find your *logos,* and you are ready to round out your essay and set it spinning.

The central idea, or thesis, is your essay's life and spirit. If your thesis is sufficiently firm and clear, it may tell you immediately how to organize your supporting material and so obviate elaborate planning. If you do not find a thesis, your essay will be a tour through the miscellaneous. An essay replete with scaffolds and catwalks—"We have just seen this; now let us turn to this"—is an essay in which the inherent idea is weak or nonexistent. A purely expository and descriptive essay, one simply about "Cats," for instance, will have to rely on outer scaffolding alone (some orderly progression from Persia to Siam) since it really has no idea at all. It is all subject, all cats, instead of being based on an idea *about* cats.

THE ARGUMENTATIVE EDGE

Find your thesis.
The *about*-ness puts an argumentative edge on the subject. When you have something to say *about* cats, you have found your underly-

ing idea. You have something to defend, something to fight about: not just "Cats," but "The cat is really a person's best friend." Now the hackles on all dog people are rising, and you have an argument on your hands. You have something to prove. You have a thesis.

The more unpopular the viewpoint and the stronger the push against convention, the stronger the thesis and the more energetic the essay. Compare the energy in "Democracy is good" with that in "Communism is good." The first is filled with platitudes; the second, with plutonium. By the same token, if you can find the real energy in "Democracy is good," if you can get down through the sand to where the roots and water are, you will have a real essay. The opposition against which you generate your energy is the heaviest in the world: boredom.

To find a thesis and to put it into one sentence is to narrow and define your subject to a workable size. Under "Cats," you must deal with all felinity from the jungle up, carefully partitioning the eons and areas, the tigers and tabbies, the sizes and shapes. The minute you proclaim the cat the friend of humanity, you have pared away whole categories and chapters, and need only think up the arguments sufficient to overwhelm the opposition. So, put an *argumentative edge* on your subject — and you will have found your thesis.

Simple exposition, to be sure, has its uses. You may want to tell someone how to build a doghouse, how to can asparagus, how to follow the outlines of relativity, or even how to write an essay. Writing a few paragraphs of straight exposition will certainly sharpen your insight into the problems of finding orderly sequences, of considering how best to lead your readers, of writing clearly and accurately. It will also suggest how much clearer an argument is.

You will see that picking an argument immediately simplifies the problems so troublesome in straight exposition: the defining, the partitioning, the narrowing of the subject. Not that you must be constantly pugnacious or aggressive. I have overstated my point to make it stick. Actually, you can put an argumentative edge on the flattest of expository subjects. "How to build a doghouse" might become "Building a doghouse is a thorough introduction to the building trades, including architecture and mechanical engineering." "Canning asparagus" might become "An asparagus patch is a course in economics." "Relativity" might become "Relativity is not so inscrutable as many suppose." Literary subjects take an argumentative edge almost by nature. You simply assert what the essential point of a poem or play seems to be: "*Hamlet* is essentially about a world that has lost its values." You assume that your readers are in search of clarity, that you have a loyal opposition consisting of the interested but uninformed. You have given your subject its edge; you have limited and organized it at a single stroke. Pick an argument, then— even a very quiet argument—and you will automatically be defining and narrowing your subject, and all the partitions you don't need will fold up. Instead of dealing with things, subjects, and pieces of subjects, you will be dealing with an idea and its consequences.

Sharpen your thesis.

Take a stand, make a judgment of value. Be reasonable, but don't be timid. It is helpful to think of your thesis, your main idea, as a debating question—"Resolved: Welfare payments must go"—taking out the "Resolved" when you actually write your thesis down. But your resolution will be even stronger, your essay clearer and tighter, if you can sharpen your thesis even further—"Resolved: Welfare payments must go because _____." Fill in that blank, and your worries are practically over. The main idea is to put your whole argument into one sentence.

Try, for instance: "Welfare payments must go because they are making people irresponsible." I don't know at all if that is true, and neither will you until you write your way into it, considering probabilities and alternatives and objections, and especially the underlying assumptions. The basic assumption—that irresponsibility is growing—may be entirely false. But you can put your well-honed thesis-sentence on a card on the wall in front of you to keep from drifting off target. You will now want to dress it for the public, to make it comely. Suppose you try:

> **Welfare payments, perhaps more than anything else, are eroding personal initiative.**

But is this fully true? Perhaps you had better try something like:

> **Despite their immediate benefits, welfare payments may actually be eroding personal initiative and depriving society of needed workers.**

This is really your thesis, and you can write that down on a scrap of paper too.

Believe in your thesis.

Notice how your original assertion has mellowed as you have brought it under critical inspection. You have asked yourself what is true in it: what can (and cannot) be assumed true, what can (and cannot) be proved true. And you have asked yourself where you stand.

You should, indeed, look for a thesis you believe in, something you can even get enthusiastic about. Arguing on both sides of a question, as debaters do, is no doubt good exercise, if one can stand it. It breaks up old ground and uncovers what you can and do believe, at least for the moment. But the argument without the belief will be hollow. So begin with what you believe, and explore its validities.

Conversely, you must test your belief with all the objections you can think of, just as you have already tested your first proposition about welfare payments. First, you have acknowledged the most evident objection—that the opposition's view must have some merit—by starting your final version with "Despite their immediate benefits . . . ." Second, you have gone a little deeper by seeing that in your bold previous version you had, with the words *are eroding,* begged the question of whether responsibility is in fact undergoing erosion; that is, you had silently assumed that responsibility *is* being eroded. This is one of the oldest fallacies and tricks of logic. To "beg the question," by error or intent, is to take for granted that which the opposition has not granted, to assume as already proved that which is yet to be proved. But you have saved yourself. You have changed *are eroding* to *may be eroding.* You have gone further in deleting the *perhaps more than anything else.* You have come closer to the truth.

You may wonder if it is not astoundingly presumptuous to go around stating theses before you have studied your subject from all angles, made several house-to-house surveys, and read everything ever written. A natural uncertainty and feeling of ignorance, and a misunderstanding of what truth is, can well inhibit you from finding a thesis. But no one knows everything. No one would write anything if he waited until he did. To a great extent, the writing of a thing is the learning of it.

So, first, make a desperate thesis and get into the arena. This is probably solution enough. If it becomes increasingly clear that your thesis is untrue, no matter how hard you push it, turn it around and use the other end. If your convictions have begun to falter with:

> **Despite their immediate benefits, welfare payments undermine initiative. . . .**

try it the other way around, with something like:

> **Although welfare payments may offend the rugged individualist, they relieve much want and anxiety, and they enable many a fatherless family to maintain its integrity.**

You will now have a beautiful command of the major objections to your new position. And you will have learned something about human fallibility and the nature of truth.

Persuade your reader.

Once you believe in your proposition, you will discover that proving it is really a venture in persuasion. *Rhetoric* is, in fact, the art of persuasion, of moving the reader to your belief. You have made a thesis, a hypothesis really—an opinion as to what the truth seems to be from where you stand, with the information you have. Belief has an unfolding energy. Write what you believe. You may be wrong, of course, but you will probably discover this as you probe for reasons; you can then reverse your thesis, pointed with your new conviction. The truth remains true, and you must at least glimpse it before you can begin to persuade others to see it. So follow your convictions, and think up reasons to convince your reader. Give him enough evidence to persuade him that what you say is probably true; find arguments that will stand up in the marketplace and survive the public haggle. You must find public reasons for your private convictions.

Don't apologize.

"In my opinion," the beginner will write repeatedly, until he seems to be saying "It is only *my* opinion, after all, so it can't be worth much." He has failed to realize that his whole essay represents his opinion—of what the truth of the matter is. Don't make your essay into a diary, or a letter to Parent or Teacher, a confidential report of what happened to you last night as you agonized over a certain question. "*To me,* Robert Frost is a great poet"—this is really writing about yourself. You are only confessing private convictions. To find the "public reasons" often requires no more than a trick of grammar: a shift from "*To me,* Robert Frost is . . ." to "Robert Frost is . . . ," from "*I thought* the poem *meant* . . ." to "The poem *means* . . . ," from you and your room last night to your subject and what it *is*. The grammatical shift represents a whole change of viewpoint, from self to subject. You become the informed adult, showing the reader around firmly, politely, and persuasively.

Once you have effaced yourself from your thesis, once you have erased *to me* and *in my opinion* and all such signs of amateur terror, you may later let yourself back into the essay for emphasis or graciousness: "Mr. Watson errs, I think, precisely at this point." You can thus ease your most tentative or violent assertions, and show that you are polite and sensible, reasonably sure of your position but aware of the possibility of error. Again: the reasonable adult. But it is better to omit the "I" altogether than to write a junior auto-biography of your discoveries and doubts.

Plan to rewrite!

As you write your weekly assignments and find your voice, you will also be learning to groom your thoughts, to present them clearly and fully, to make sure you have said what you thought you said. Good writing comes only from rewriting. Even your happy thoughts will need resetting, as you join them to the frequently happier ones that a second look seems to call up. Even the letter-perfect paper will improve almost of itself if you simply sit down to type it through again. You will find, almost unbidden, sharper words, better phrases, new figures of speech, and new illustrations and ideas to replace the weedy patches not noticed before. So, *allow yourself time for revision*.

Now, with clear conscience, you are ready to write. Your single thesis sentence has conjured up your essay; all you need now is some form to put it in.

EXERCISES

1 Pick three of four of the following general subjects and convert them into debating resolutions ("Resolved: Cats make better pets than dogs"; "Resolved: Welfare must go"):

marijuana	foreign languages
violence	abortion
fraternities	the inner city
grades	medical care
ecology	communes
athletics	textbooks

2 Now drop the "Resolved" and add a "because _____" to each ("Welfare must go because it is making people irresponsible").

3 Now smooth out these theses for public appearance, omitting the direct statement of *because* and adding qualifications ("Despite its many advantages, welfare may actually be eroding our heritage of personal responsibility").

4 Now turn your smoothed theses completely around, so that they assert the opposite ("Although welfare may offend the rugged individualist, it relieves much want and anxiety while promoting a sense of shared responsibility").

Two
Structure

BEGINNING, MIDDLE, END

As Aristotle long ago pointed out, works that spin their way through time need a beginning, a middle, and an end to give them the stability of spatial things like paintings and statues. You need a clear beginning to give your essay character and direction so the reader can tell where he is going and can look forward with expectation. Your beginning, of course, will set forth your thesis. You need a middle to amplify and fulfill. This will be the body of your argument, the bulk of your essay. You need an end to let readers know that they have arrived and where. This will be your final paragraph, a summation and reassertion of your theme.

Give your essay the three-part *feel* of beginning, middle, and end — the mind likes this triple order. Many a freshman's essay has no structure and leaves no impression. It is all chaotic middle. It has no beginning, it just starts; it has no end, it just stops, fagged out at two in the morning.

The beginning must feel like a beginning, not just like an accident. It should be at least a full paragraph that lets your reader gently into the subject and culminates with your thesis. The end, likewise, should be a full paragraph, one that drives the point home, pushes the implications wide, and brings the reader to rest, back on the fundamental thesis to give a sense of completion. When we consider paragraphing in the next chapter, we will look more closely at beginning paragraphs and end paragraphs. The "middle" of your essay, which constitutes its bulk, needs further structural consideration now.

MIDDLE TACTICS

Arrange your points in order of increasing interest.

Once your thesis has sounded the challenge, your reader's interest is probably at its highest pitch. He wants to see how you can prove so outrageous a thing, or to see what the arguments are for this thing he has always believed but never tested. Each step of the way into your demonstration, he is learning more of what you have to say. But, unfortunately, his interest may be relaxing as it becomes satisfied: the reader's normal line of attention is a progressive decline, arching down like a wintry graph. Against this decline you must oppose your forces, making each successive point more interesting. And save your best till last. It is as simple as that.

Here, for example, is the middle of a short, three-paragraph essay developing the thesis that "Working your way through college is valuable." The student has arranged his three points in an ascending order of interest:

> The student who works finds that the experience is worth more than the money. First, he learns to budget his time. He now supports himself by using time he would otherwise waste, and he studies harder in the time he has left because he knows it is limited. Second, he makes real and lasting friends on the job, as compared to the other casual acquaintances around the campus. He has shared rush hours, and nighttime cleanups with the dishes piled high, and conversation and jokes when business is slow. Finally, he gains confidence in his ability to get along with all kinds of people, and to make his own way. He sees how businesses operate, and how waitresses, for instance, can work cheerfully at a really tiring job without much hope for the future. He gains an insight into the real world, which is a good contrast to the more intellectual and idealistic world of the college student.

Again, each successive item of your presentation should be more interesting than the last, or you will suddenly seem anticlimactic. Actually, minor regressions of interest make no difference so long as the whole tendency is uphill and your last item clearly the best. Suppose, for example, you were to undertake the cat thesis. You decide that four points would make up the case, and that you might arrange them in the following order of increasing interest: (1) cats are affectionate but make few demands; (2) cats actually look out for themselves; (3) cats have, in fact, proved extremely useful to society throughout history in controlling mice and other plaguy rodents; (4) cats satisfy some human need for a touch of the jungle, savagery in repose, ferocity in silk, and have been worshiped for the exotic power they still seem to represent. It may be, as you write, that you will find Number 1 developing attractive or amusing instances, and perhaps even virtually usurping the whole essay. Numbers 2, 3, and 4 should then be moved ahead as interesting but brief preliminaries. Your middle structure, thus, should range from least important to most important, from simple to complex, from narrow to broad, from pleasant to hilarious, from mundane to metaphysical — whatever "leasts" and "mosts" your subject suggests.

Acknowledge and dispose of the opposition, point by point.

Your cat essay, because it is moderately playful, can proceed rather directly, throwing only an occasional bone of concession to the dogs, and perhaps most of your essays, as you discuss the Constitutional Convention or explain a poem, will have little opposition to worry about. But a serious controversial argument demands one organizational consideration beyond the simple structure of ascending interest. Although you have taken your stand firmly as a *pro,* you will have to allow scope to the *con*'s, or you will seem not to have thought much about your subject. The more opposition you can manage as you carry your point, the more triumphant you will seem, like a high-wire artist daring the impossible.

This balancing of *pro*'s against *con*'s is one of the most fundamental orders of thought: the dialectic order, which is the order of argument, one side pitted against the other. Our minds naturally swing from side to side as we think. In dialectics, we simply give one side an argumentative edge, producing a thesis that cuts a clear line through any subject: "This is better than that." The basic organizing principle here is to get rid of the opposition first, and to end on your own side. Probably you will have already organized your thesis sentence in a perfect pattern for your *con-pro* argument:

> **Despite their many advantages, welfare payments . . . .**
> **Although dogs are fine pets, cats . . . .**

The subordinate clause (see p. 48) states the subordinate part of your argument, which is your concession to the *con* viewpoint; your main clause states your main argument. As the subordinate clause comes first in your thesis sentence, so with the subordinate argument in your essay. Sentence and essay both reflect a natural psychological principle. You want, and the reader wants, to get the opposition out of the way. And you want to end on your best foot. (You might try putting the opposition last, just to see how peculiarly the last word insists on seeming best, and how, when stated last by you, the opposition's case seems to be your own.)

Get rid of the opposition first. This is the essential tactic of argumentation. You have introduced and stated your thesis in your beginning paragraph. Now start the middle with a paragraph of concession to the *con*'s:

> **Dog-lovers, of course, have tradition on their side. Dogs are indeed affectionate and faithful. . . .**

And with that paragraph out of the way, go to bat for the cats, showing their superiority to dogs in every point. In a very brief essay, you can use the opposition itself to introduce your thesis in the first paragraph, and dispose of your opponents at the same time:

> **Shakespeare begins *Romeo and Juliet* with ominous warnings about fate. His lovers are "star-crossed," he says: they are doomed from the first by their contrary stars, by the universe itself. They have sprung from "fatal loins." Fate has already determined their tragic end. The play then unfolds a succession of unlucky and presumably fated accidents. Nevertheless, we soon discover that Shakespeare really blames the tragedy not on fate but on human stupidity and error.**

But usually your beginning paragraph will lead up to your thesis more or less neutrally, and you will attack your opposition head-on in paragraph two, as you launch into the middle.

If the opposing arguments seem relatively slight and brief, you can get rid of them neatly all together in one paragraph before you get down to your case. Immediately after your beginning, which has stated your thesis, you write a paragraph of concession: "Of course, security is a good thing. No one wants people begging." And so on to the end of the paragraph, deflating every conceivable objection. Then back to the main line: "But the price in moral decay is too great." The structure of the paragraph might be diagramed something like the scheme shown in Diagram I (next page).

If the opposition is more considerable, demolish it point by point, using a series of *con*'s and *pro*'s, in two or three paragraphs, before you steady down to your own side. Each paragraph can be a small argument that presents the opposition, then knocks it flat—a kind of Punch-and-Judy show: "We must admit that . . . . But . . . ." And down goes the poor old opposition again. Or you could swing your argument through a number of alternating paragraphs: first

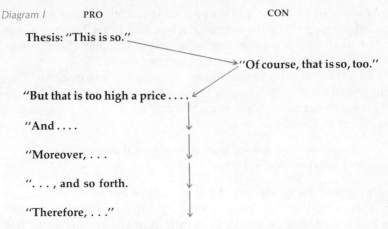

Diagram I   PRO   CON

your beginning, the thesis, then a paragraph to the opposition *(con)*, then one for your side *(pro)*, then another paragraph of *con*, and so on. The main point, again, is this: get rid of the opposition first. One paragraph of concession right after your thesis will probably handle most of your adversaries, and the more complicated argumentative swingers, like the one diagramed on the facing page, will develop naturally as you need them.

You will notice that *but* and *however* are always guides for the *pro*'s, serving as switches back to the main line. *But, however,* and *Nevertheless* are the basic *pro*'s. *But* always heads its turning sentence (not followed by a comma); *Nevertheless* usually does (followed by a comma). I am sure, however, that *however* is always better buried in the sentence between commas. "However, . . ." is the habit of heavy prose. *But* is for the quick turn; the inlaid *however* for the more elegant sweep.

The structural line of your arguments, then, might look like Diagram II, and an actual *pro-con* argument like Diagram III (p. 14).

Comparing and contrasting two poems, two stories, two ball players, are further instances of this essential process of thought, of this important way to understanding. You may wish simply to set two similars, or dissimilars, side by side to illustrate some larger point—that excellence may come in very different packages, for instance. Comparing and contrasting can illuminate the unfamiliar with the familiar, or it can help you discover and convey to your readers new perspectives on things well known—two popular singers, two of Shakespeare's sonnets, two nursery rhymes. But, whether or not you are presenting one side as superior to the other, the structural tactic is the same: compare point for point, so long as the comparison illuminates.

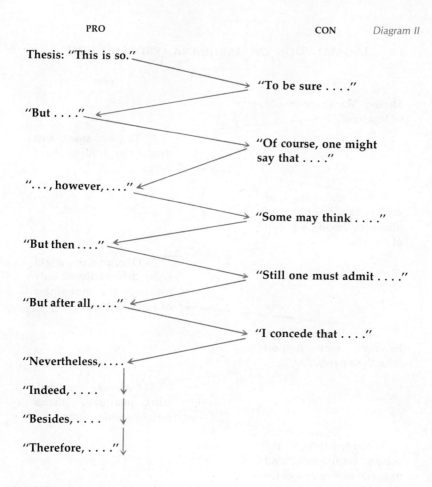

PRO   CON   *Diagram II*

Thesis: "This is so."

                                   "To be sure . . . ."

"But . . . ."

                                   "Of course, one might
say that . . . ."

". . . , however, ..."

                                   "Some may think . . . ."

"But then . . . ."

                                   "Still one must admit . . . ."

"But after all, ..."

                                   "I concede that . . . ."

"Nevertheless, ...

"Indeed, ...

"Besides, ...

"Therefore, ..."

EXERCISES

1 In the following exercise you will find groups of information and ideas haphazardly arranged. Rewrite the statements with the information arranged in an ascending order of interest and importance. Then, in a sentence or two, explain your reasons for using that order.

  1. We are now being made to realize the negative aspects of the technological "progress" of the twentieth century: 50,000 highway deaths per year, air and water pollution, the population explosion, nuclear warfare, loss of privacy.

  2. The psychological effects of the Recession are observable in an increase in the frequency of mental breakdown, an increase in the suicide rate, and a decrease in the birth rate.

Diagram III

LEGALIZATION OF MARIJUANA – PRO AND CON

PRO   CON

Thesis: "Marijuana should
be legalized."

                                   To be sure, soft
drugs can lead to hard
drugs. . . .

But most users of
marijuana seek only mild
pleasures among a group
of friends. . . .

                                   Of course, one might
argue that marijuana only
prolongs the groupiness
of adolescence. . . .

People at every age,
however, seek support
from their peers. . . .

                                   I concede that legal-
izing marijuana invites
certain serious risks. . . .

Nevertheless, the
present punishment and
its social consequences far
exceed these risks. . . .

Indeed, the law
could eliminate many dan-
gers by controlling quality.
. . .

Besides, legality
would eliminate the
profiteers. . . .

Therefore, legalizing
marijuana would solve
more problems than its
illegality now creates. . . .

3. An all-volunteer army may be undesirable because it tends to draw from a limited segment of the population, to create an elitist military caste such as those in Hitler's Germany and in tsarist Russia, and to cost more. But it does away with the draft.

4. If you have gotten along without a credit card until now, applying for one is really a mistake. If you have one, you might lose it or have it stolen, and then you might be liable for the expenses run up by someone else using your card. Then there are the interest charges. Few people realize that the interest on most credit cards is 18 percent a year. And obviously, if you have a credit card, you are going to spend more than if you were using cash.

5. Talking about scientific knowledge today, she identified three of its characteristics. First, this knowledge is not within the reach of most of us. Second, this knowledge is mostly new. And, finally, this knowledge has become almost the exclusive property of a very small group of scientists and engineers.

2 Take a popular proposition, like "Grades are unnecessary," "Cars should be barred from central cities," or "Throw-away bottles should be abolished," and write down three or four supporting arguments, ones that would really stick. Arrange your items in order of increasing interest.

3 Choose a thesis to cover the following points (for or against public transportation, for instance). Then, underneath your thesis, list these points in an order of ascending interest, and in a *pro-con* structure, adding necessary *but*'s and *of course*'s and so forth, and other intermediate points of your own:

> The automobile pollutes the atmosphere.
> Public transportation is going bankrupt.
> The economy requires obsolescence.
> Cars were once built to last.
> A car is a necessity.

4 Write an outline of a comparative argument. State your thesis; then simply list your points in order of increasing interest, phrasing them in the general pattern of "Painting is fun, but sculpture is better."

Three
Paragraphs

THE STANDARD PARAGRAPH

A paragraph is a structural convenience—a building block to get firmly in mind. I mean the standard, central paragraph, setting aside for the moment the peculiarly shaped beginning paragraph and ending paragraph. You build the bulk of your essay with standard paragraphs, with blocks of concrete ideas, and they should fit smoothly. But they should also remain as perceptible parts, to rest your reader's eye and mind. Indeed, the paragraph originated, among the Greeks, as a resting place and place-finder, being first a mere mark (*graphos*) in the margin alongside (*para*) an unbroken sheet of handwriting— the proofreader's familiar ¶. You have heard that a paragraph is a single idea, and this is true. But so is a word, usually; and so is a sentence, sometimes. It seems best, after all, to think of a paragraph as something you use for your reader's convenience, rather than as some granitic form laid down by molten logic.

The writing medium determines the size of the paragraph. Your average longhand paragraph may look the same size to you as a typewritten one, and both may seem the same size as a paragraph in a book. But the printed page might show your handwritten paragraph so short as to be embarrassing, and your typewritten paragraph barely long enough for decency. Handwriting plus typewriting plus insecurity equals inadequate paragraphs. Your first impulse may be to write little paragraphs, often only a sentence to each. If so, you are not yet writing in any medium at all.

Journalists, of course, are habitually one-sentence paragraphers. The narrowness of the newspaper column makes a sentence look like a paragraph, and narrow columns and short paragraphs serve the rapid transit for which newspapers are designed. A paragraph from a book might fill a whole newspaper column with solid lead. It would have to be broken—paragraphed—for the reader's convenience. On the other hand, a news story on the page of a book would look like a gap-toothed comb, and would have to be consolidated for the reader's comfort.

Plan for the big paragraph.

Imagine yourself writing for print, but in a book, not a newspaper. Force yourself to four or five sentences at least, visualizing your paragraphs as about all of a size. Think of them as identical rectangular frames to be filled. This will allow you to build with orderly blocks, to strengthen your feel for structure. Since the beginner's problem is usually one of thinking of things to say rather than of trimming the overgrowth, you can do your filling out a unit at a time, always thinking up one or two sentences more to fill the customary space. You will probably be repetitive and wordy at first —this is our universal failing—but you will soon learn to fill your paragraph with clean and interesting details. You will get to feel a kind of constructional rhythm as you find yourself coming to a resting place at the end of your customary paragraphic frame.

Once accustomed to a five-sentence frame, say, you can then begin to vary the length for emphasis, letting a good idea swell out beyond the norm, or bringing a particular point home in a paragraph short and sharp—even in one sentence, like this.

The paragraph's structure, then, has its own rhetorical message. It tells the reader visually whether or not you are in charge of your subject and are leading him confidently to see what you already know. Tiny, ragged paragraphs display your hidden uncertainty, unless clearly placed among big ones for emphasis. Brief opening and closing paragraphs sometimes can emphasize your thesis effectively, but usually they make your beginning seem hasty and your ending perfunctory. So aim for the big paragraph all the way, and vary it only occasionally and knowingly, for rhetorical emphasis.

Find a topic sentence.

Looked at as a convenient structural frame, the paragraph reveals a further advantage. Like the essay itself, it has a beginning, a middle, and an end. The beginning and the end are usually each one sentence long, and the middle gets you smoothly from one to the other. Since, like the essay, the paragraph flows through time, its last sentence is the most emphatic. This is your home punch. The first sentence holds the next most emphatic place. It will normally be your *topic sentence,* stating the small thesis of a miniature essay, something like this:

> *Jefferson believed in democracy because of his fearless belief in reason.* He knew that reason was far from perfect, but he also knew that it was the best faculty we have. He knew that it was better than all the frightened and angry intolerances with which we fence off our own back yards at the cost of injustice. Thought must be free. Discussion must be free. Reason must be free to range among the widest possibilities. Even the opinion we hate, and have reasons for believing wrong, we must leave free so that reason can operate on it, so that we advertise our belief in reason and demonstrate a faith unafraid of the consequences — because we know that the consequences will be right. Freedom is really not the aim and end of Jeffersonian democracy: freedom is the means by which democracy can rationally choose justice for all.

If your topic sentence covers everything within your paragraph, your paragraph is coherent, and you are using your paragraphs with maximum effect, leading your reader into your community block by block. If your end sentences bring him briefly to rest, he will know where he is and appreciate it.

BEGINNING PARAGRAPHS: THE FUNNEL

State your thesis at the END of your beginning paragraph.

Your beginning paragraph should contain your main idea, and present it to best advantage. Its topic sentence is also the *thesis sentence* of your entire essay. The clearest and most emphatic place for your thesis sentence is at the *end* — not at the beginning — of the beginning paragraph. If you put it first, you will have to repeat some version of it as you bring your beginning paragraph to a close. If you put it in the middle, the reader will very likely take something else as your main point, probably whatever the last sentence contains. The inevitable psychology of interest, as you move your reader through your first paragraph and into your essay, urges you to put your thesis last — in the last sentence of your beginning paragraph.

Think of your beginning paragraph, then, not as a frame to be filled, but as a funnel. Start wide and end narrow:

OPENING   INVITATION

THESIS

If, for instance, you wished to show that learning to play the guitar pays off in friendship, you would start somewhere back from your specific thesis with something more general — about music, about learning, about the pleasures of achievement, about guitars: "Playing the guitar looks easy," "Music can speak more directly than words," "Learning anything is a course in frustration." You can even open with something quite specific, *as long as it is more general than your thesis:* "Pick up a guitar, and you bump into people." As you can see from these examples, a handy way to find an opener is to take one word from your thesis — *learning, play,* or *guitar,* for instance — and make a sentence out of it. Say something about it, and you are well on your way to your thesis, three or four sentences later.* This will keep you from starting too far back, and losing your reader in puddles of platitudes: "Everyone likes to be popular. Most people like music . . . ." Your opening line, in other words, should clearly look forward to your thesis, should be something to engage interest easily, something to which most readers would assent without a rise in blood pressure. (Antagonize and startle if you wish, but beware of having the door slammed before you have a chance, and of making your thesis an anticlimax.) Therefore: broad and genial. From your opening geniality, you move progressively down to smaller particulars. You narrow down: from learning the guitar, to its musical and social complications, to its rewards in friendship (your thesis).

* I am grateful to James C. Raymond, of the University of Alabama, for this helpful idea.

Your paragraph might run, from broad to narrow, like this:

> Learning anything has unexpected rocks in its path, but the guitar seems particularly rocky. It looks so simple. A few chords, you think, and you are on your way. Then you discover not only the musical and technical difficulties, but a whole unexpected crowd of human complications. Your friends think you are showing off; the people you meet think you are a fake. Then the frustrations drive you to achievement. You learn to face the music and the people honestly. You finally learn to play a little, but you also discover something better. You have learned to make and keep some real friends, because you have discovered a kind of ultimate friendship with yourself.

Now, that paragraph turned out a little different from what I anticipated. I overshot my original thesis, discovering, as I wrote, a thesis one step farther—an underlying cause—about coming to friendly terms with oneself. But it illustrates the funnel, from the broad and general to the one particular point that will be your essay's main idea, your thesis. Here is another example:

> The environment is the world around us, and everyone agrees it needs a cleaning. Big corporations gobble up the countryside and disgorge what's left into the breeze and streams. Big trucks rumble by, trailing their fumes. A jet roars into the air, and its soot drifts over the trees. Everyone calls for massive action, and then tosses away his cigarette butt or gum wrapper. The world around us is also a sidewalk, a lawn, a lounge, a hallway, a room right here. Cleaning the environment can begin by reaching for the scrap of paper at your feet.

MIDDLE PARAGRAPHS

Make your middle paragraphs full, and use transitions.

The middle paragraph is the standard paragraph, the little essay in itself, with its own little beginning and little end. But it must also declare its allegiance to the paragraphs immediately before and after it. Each topic sentence must somehow hook onto the paragraph above it, must include some word or phrase to ease the reader's path: a transition. You may simply repeat a word from the sentence that ended the paragraph just above. You may bring down a thought left slightly hanging in air: "Smith's idea is different" might be a tremendously economical topic sentence with automatic transition. Or you may get from one paragraph to the next by the usual steppingstones, like *but, however, nevertheless, therefore, indeed, of course.*

One brief transitional touch in your topic sentence is usually sufficient.

The topic sentences in each of the following three paragraphs by James Baldwin contain neat transitions. I have just used an old standby myself: repeating the words *topic sentence* from the close of my preceding paragraph. Baldwin has just described the young people of Harlem who have given up, escaping into day-long TV, or the local bar, or drugs. He now begins his next paragraph with *And the others,* a strong and natural transition, referring back, reinforced with the further transitional reference *all of these deaths.* In the next paragraph, *them* does the trick; in the last, *other* again makes the transition and sets the contrast. The paragraphs are nearly the same length, all cogent, clear, and full. No one-sentence paragraphing here, no gaps, but all a vivid, orderly progression:

> <u>And the others</u>, who have avoided <u>all of these deaths</u>, get up in the morning and go downtown to meet "the man." They work in the white man's world all day and come home in the evening to this fetid block. They struggle to instill in their children some private sense of honor or dignity which will help the child to survive. This means, of course, that they must struggle, stolidly, incessantly, to keep this sense alive in themselves, in spite of the insults, the indifference, and the cruelty they are certain to encounter in their working day. They patiently browbeat the landlord into fixing the heat, the plaster, the plumbing; this demands prodigious patience; nor is patience usually enough. In trying to make their hovels habitable, they are perpetually throwing good money after bad. Such frustration, so long endured, is driving many strong, admirable men and women whose only crime is color to the very gates of paranoia.
>
> One remembers <u>them</u> from another time—playing handball in the playground, going to church, wondering if they were going to be promoted at school. One remembers them going off to war —gladly, to escape this block. One remembers their return. Perhaps one remembers their wedding day. And one sees where the girl is now—vainly looking for salvation from some other embittered, trussed, and struggling boy—and sees the all-but-abandoned children in the streets.
>
> Now I am perfectly aware that there are <u>other</u> slums in which white men are fighting for their lives, and mainly losing. I know that blood is also flowing through those streets and that the human damage there is incalculable. People are continually pointing out to me the wretchedness of white people in order to console me for the wretchedness of blacks. But an itemized account of the American failure does not console me and it should not console anyone else. That hundreds of thousands of white people are liv-

ing, in effect, no better than the "niggers" is not a fact to be regarded with complacency. The social and moral bankruptcy suggested by this fact is of the bitterest, most terrifying kind.*

Here are the four points to remember about middle paragraphs. First, think of the middle paragraph as a miniature essay, with a beginning, a middle, and an end. Its beginning will normally be its topic sentence, the thesis of this miniature essay. Its middle will develop, explain, and illustrate your topic sentence. Its last sentence will drive home the idea. Second, see that your paragraph is coherent, not only flowing smoothly but with nothing in it not covered by the topic sentence. Third, make your paragraphs full and well developed, with plenty of details, examples, and full explanations, or you will end up with a skeletal paper with very little meat on its bones. Fourth, remember transitions. Though each paragraph is a kind of miniature essay, it is also a part of a larger essay. Therefore, hook each paragraph smoothly to the paragraph preceding it, with some transitional touch in each topic sentence.

END PARAGRAPHS: THE INVERTED FUNNEL

Reassert your thesis.
If the beginning paragraph is a funnel, the end paragraph is a funnel upside down: the thought starts moderately narrow—it is more or less the thesis you have had all the time—and then pours out broader and broader implications and finer emphases. The end paragraph reiterates, summarizes, and emphasizes with decorous fervor. This is your last chance. This is what your readers will carry away—and if you can carry *them* away, so much the better. All within decent intellectual bounds, of course. You are the person of reason still, but the person of reason supercharged with conviction, sure of your idea and sure of its importance.

The final paragraph conveys a sense of assurance and repose, of business completed. Its topic sentence should be some version of your original thesis sentence, since the end paragraph is the exact structural opposite and complement of the beginning one. Its transitional word or phrase is often one of finality or summary—*then, finally, thus,* and *so:*

* From "Fifth Avenue Uptown: A Letter from Harlem," in *Nobody Knows My Name* (New York: Dial Press, 1961), pp. 59–61. Copyright © 1960 by James Baldwin. Reprinted by permission of Dial Press. (Originally published in *Esquire.*)

So, the guitar is a means to a finer end.
The environment, then, is in our lungs and at our fingertips.

The paragraph would then proceed to expand and elaborate this re-vived thesis. We would get a confident assertion that both the music and the friendships are really by-products of an inner alliance; we would get an urgent plea to clean up our personal environs and strengthen our convictions. One rule of thumb: the longer the paper, the more specific the summary of the points you have made. A short paper will need no specific summary of your points at all; the re-newed thesis and its widening of implications are sufficient.

Here is an end paragraph by Sir James Jeans. His transitional phrase is *for a similar reason*. His thesis was that previous concepts of physical reality had mistaken surfaces for depths:

> The purely mechanical picture of visible nature fails for a sim-ilar reason. It proclaims that the ripples themselves direct the work-ings of the universe instead of being mere symptoms of occurrences below; in brief, it makes the mistake of thinking that the weather-vane determines the direction from which the wind shall blow, or that the thermometer keeps the room hot.*

In the following end paragraph of Richard Hofstadter's his tran-sitional word is *intellectuals,* carried over from the preceding para-graphs. His thesis was that intellectuals should not abandon their defense of intellectual and spiritual freedom, as they have tended to do, under pressure to conform:

> This world will never be governed by intellectuals — it may rest assured. But *we* must be assured, too, that intellectuals will not be altogether governed by this world, that they maintain their piety, their longstanding allegiance to the world of spiritual val-ues to which they should belong. Otherwise there will be no in-tellectuals, at least not above ground. And societies in which the intellectuals have been driven underground, as we have had occa-sion to see in our own time, are societies in which even the anti-intellectuals are unhappy.†

* *The New Background of Science* (Cambridge: Cambridge University Press, 1933), p. 261.

† "Democracy and Anti-intellectualism in America," *Michigan Quarterly Review*, 59 (1953), 295.

THE WHOLE ESSAY

You have now discovered the main ingredients of a good essay. You have learned to find and to sharpen your thesis in one sentence, to give your essay that all-important argumentative edge. You have learned to arrange your points in order of increasing interest, and you have practiced disposing of the opposition in a *pro-con* structure. You have seen that your beginning paragraph should look like a funnel, working from broad generalization to thesis. You have tried your hand at middle paragraphs, which are almost like little essays with their own beginnings and ends. And finally, you have learned that your last paragraph should work like an inverted funnel, broadening and embellishing your thesis.

Some students have pictured the essay as a Greek column, with a narrowing beginning paragraph as its top, or capital, and a broadening end paragraph as its base. Others have seen it as a keyhole, (see the diagram opposite). But either way, you should see a structure, with solid beginning and end, supported by a well-shaped middle.

The three-paragraph essay that follows illustrates the "keyhole" structure. The first sentence, "If you drive out west . . . ," is the "opening invitation;" the first paragraph funnels to ". . . you will realize that the answer is cattle," the first statement of the essay's thesis. The middle paragraph is the entire middle, or body, of the essay. Beginning with the topic sentence, "These towns were the destinations . . . ," increasingly stronger points lead to the strongest, contained in the phrase "with the towns spreading northward behind the businesses." Then the first sentence of the third, and end, paragraph rewords the thesis: "The cattle business itself shaped these one-sided Nebraska towns." Generalizations follow, taking the reader through the inverted funnel of the last paragraph to the "clincher," the point of the essay itself: ". . . the great herds of the old Southwest, together with the transcontinental railroad and man's need to make a living, plotted these Western towns north of the tracks."

North of the Tracks

If you drive out west from Chicago, you will notice something happening to the towns. After the country levels into Nebraska, the smaller towns are built only on one side of the road. When you stop for a rest, and look south across the broad main street, you will see the railroad immediately beyond. All of these towns spread northward from the tracks. Why? As you munch your hamburger

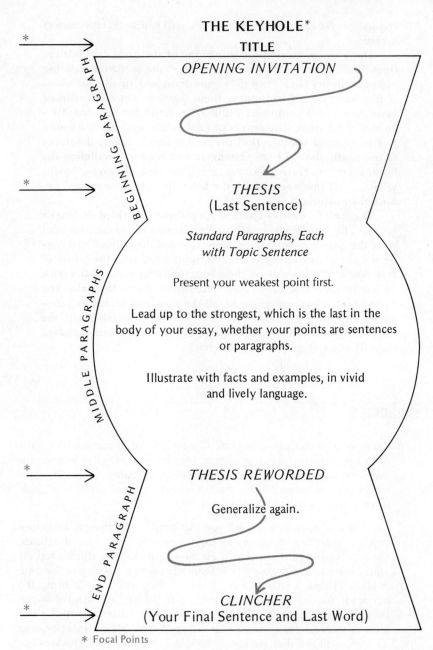

THE KEYHOLE*
TITLE

OPENING INVITATION

BEGINNING PARAGRAPH

THESIS
(Last Sentence)

Standard Paragraphs, Each with Topic Sentence

MIDDLE PARAGRAPHS

Present your weakest point first.

Lead up to the strongest, which is the last in the body of your essay, whether your points are sentences or paragraphs.

Illustrate with facts and examples, in vivid and lively language.

THESIS REWORDED

Generalize again.

END PARAGRAPH

CLINCHER
(Your Final Sentence and Last Word)

* Focal Points

*Mrs. Fran Measley of Santa Barbara, California, has devised for her students this mimeographed sheet to accompany my discussion of structure and paragraphing —to help them to visualize my points through a keyhole, as it were. I am grateful to Mrs. Measley to be able to include it here.

and look at the restaurant's murals, you will realize that the answer is cattle.

These towns were the destinations of the great cattle-drives from Texas. They probably had begun at the scattered watering places in the dry land. Then the wagon-trails and, finally, the transcontinental railroad had strung them together. Once the railroad came, the whole southwest could raise cattle for the slaughterhouses of Chicago. The droves of cattle came up from the south, and all of these towns reflect the traffic: corrals beside the tracks to the south, the road for passengers and wagons paralleling the tracks on the northern side, then, along the road, the row of hotels, saloons, and businesses, with the town spreading northward behind the businesses.

The cattle business itself shaped these one-sided Nebraska towns. The conditions in which this immediate cause took root were the growing population in the East and the railroad that connected the plains of the West, and Southwest, with the tables of New York. The towns took their hopeful being north of the rails, on the leeward side of the vast cattle-drives from the south. The trade in cattle has now changed, all the way from Miami to Sacramento. But the great herds of the old Southwest, together with the transcontinental railroad and man's need to make a living, plotted these Western towns north of the tracks.

EXERCISES

1 Below is a list of thesis sentences. Choose one (or its opposite), or make one of your own on the same pattern. Then back off from it at least four or five sentences, and write a funnel-like beginning paragraph leading your reader down to it: your thesis, the last sentence of your beginning funnel. EXAMPLE, with thesis italicized, follows:

The coal operators will tell you that stripping is cheaper and more efficient than conventional mining. Their 250-cubic-yard draglines, their 200-cubic-yard shovels, their 50-ton trucks, can rip the top off a mountain and expose a whole seam of coal in a fraction of the time it takes to sink a shaft. "It is cheaper," they will say, "to bring the surface to the coal than to bring the coal to the surface." And of course they are right; in a sense it is cheaper. But visit Eastern Kentucky and look at the real price we pay for stripped coal. Visit a stripped area and you will see that, no matter how low the price for a truckload of stripped coal, *the real price for strip-mining has to be reckoned in terms of blighted land, poisoned streams, and stunted human lives.*

1. Throw-away containers are throwing away the world.

  2. Banning cigarette advertising on TV is ineffective and discriminatory.

  3. Artificial turf in football stadiums is dangerous and should be banned.

  4. If you want music, forget about tape cassettes.

  5. Legalizing off-track betting would weaken the underworld and strengthen state budgets.

2 Write an end paragraph to go with your beginning paragraph in exercise 1.

3 Write three middle paragraphs, about two hundred words each, on different subjects. Make the topic sentences cover the contents, and give each topic sentence some transitional touch: "Fly fishing *is different.*" "*But* Judaism acknowledges man as a social being." "Kennedy *also* had his blind side."

4 Write middle paragraphs for the beginning and end paragraphs in exercises 1 and 2. Did you have to alter your end paragraph because of discoveries you made in writing the middle paragraphs?

5 Expand one of the middle paragraphs you wrote for exercise 3 into a three-paragraph essay, conveying a thorough sense of beginning, middle, and end. (One of the best stylists I know, a German, told me his grasp of organization comes from having had to write, through a number of grammar-school years, nothing but three-paragraph essays. The treatment seems to have been excellent.)

Four
Description, Narration, Process

Descriptive and narrative paragraphs—showing and telling—are essential parts of argument. They frequently display our basic evidence, and they have inner organizations of their own. Describing a process, probably the commonest of expository forms, is description narrated, and here more than ever the writer's voice, his conviction, his concern for his reader's understanding, can lift the most mundane detail into functional vitality.

DESCRIPTIVE PARAGRAPHS

Put your perceptions into words.

Description is essentially *spatial*. When your subject concerns a campus, or a failing business district, you may want to write your middle as some orderly progress through space, and your paragraphs virtually as units of space: one paragraph for the intersection, one for the first building, one for the second, one for the tattered cigar store at the end of the block. Within a paragraph, you simply take your reader from one detail to the next in order. Your topic sentence summarizes the total effect: "The Whistler Building was once elegant, three stories of brick with carved stone pediments." Then your paragraph proceeds with noteworthy details in any convenient spatial order: first the sagging front door, then the windows to the left, then those to the right, then the second floor's windows, with their suggestion of dingy apartments, then those of the third, which suggest only emptiness.

The best spatial description follows the perceptions of a person entering or looking at the space described, as with the imaginary visitor in this description by R. Prawer Jhabvala of a modern house in India:

> Our foreign visitor stands agape at the wonderful residence his second host has built for himself. No expense has been spared here, no decoration suggested by a vivid taste omitted. There are little Moorish balconies and Indian domes and squiggly lattice work and an air-conditioner in every window. Inside, all is marble flooring, and in the entrance hall there is a fountain lit up with green, yellow, and red bulbs. The curtains on the windows and in the doorways are of silk, the vast sofa-suites are upholstered in velvet, the telephone is red, and huge vases are filled with plastic flowers.*

This procedure may be seen in elaborate extension, paragraph after paragraph, at the beginning of Thomas Hardy's *The Return of the Native,* in which we are moved into the setting from a great distance, as if, years before moving pictures, we are riding a cameraman's dolly.

Description frequently blends time with space, with the observer's perceptions unifying the two as he moves through them, and takes his readers with him. You pick out the striking features, showing the reader what would strike him first, as it did you, then proceeding to more minute but no less significant details. This is the usual way of describing people, as in this paragraph (by the anonymous reporter for *The New Yorker*'s "Talk of the Town") about an actual Englishman, whose odd occupation is mending the broken eggs brought to him by bird's-egg collectors:

> Colonel Prynne, who is sixty-seven, lives and carries on his singular pursuit in a rambling, thatch-roofed, five-hundred-year-old cottage in the tiny village of Spaxton, Somerset, and there, on a recent afternoon, he received us. A man of medium build who retains a military carriage, he was sprucely turned out in a brown suit, a tan jersey vest, a green shirt and tie, and tan oxfords. He has a bald, distinctly egg-shaped head, wears a close-cropped mustache and black shell-rimmed glasses, and seems always to have his nose

* *Encounter,* May 1964, pp. 42–43.

tilted slightly upward and the nostrils faintly distended, as if he were sniffing the air. After taking us on a rather cursory tour of his garden, which is as neat and well tended as its owner, he remarked crisply that it was time to get cracking, and we followed him indoors, past an enormous fireplace, which burns five-foot logs, and up a flight of stairs to a room that he calls his studio.*

You may use a descriptive paragraph to good effect in almost any kind of essay, as you illustrate by a detailed picture—the face of a town, the face of a drifter—the physical grounds for your convictions. For this, the paragraph makes an extremely convenient and coherent unit.

NARRATIVE PARAGRAPHS

Narrate to illustrate.

Time is the essence of narrative. The narrative paragraph merely exploits convenient units of time. Narrative is the primary business of fiction, of course, but occasionally an expository or argumentative essay will give over its entire middle to a narrative account of some event that illustrates its thesis. Of this kind is George Orwell's great argumentative essay "Shooting an Elephant." Orwell's thesis is that imperialism tyrannizes over the rulers as well as the ruled. To illustrate it, he tells of an incident during his career as a young police officer in Burma, when he was compelled, by the expectations of the watching crowd, to shoot a renegade elephant. Here is a narrative paragraph in which Orwell reports a crucial moment; notice how he mixes external events and snippets of conversation with his inner thoughts, pegging all perfectly with a topic sentence:

But I did not want to shoot the elephant. I watched him beating his bunch of grass against his knees, with that preoccupied grandmotherly air that elephants have. It seemed to me that it would be murder to shoot him. At that age I was not squeamish about killing animals, but I had never shot an elephant and never wanted to. (Somehow it always seems worse to kill a *large* animal.) Besides, there was the beast's owner to be considered. Alive, the elephant was worth at least a hundred pounds; dead, he would only be worth the value of his tusks, five pounds, possibly. But I had got to act quickly. I turned to some experienced-looking Burmans who had been there when we arrived, and asked them

* *The New Yorker,* May 23, 1964, p. 37.

how the elephant had been behaving. They all said the same thing:
he took no notice of you if you left him alone, but he might charge
if you went too close to him.*

Orwell is simply giving us an account of events, and of his inner
thoughts, as they happened, one after the other. Almost any kind
of essay could use a similar paragraph of narrative to illustrate a
point.

But to select details and get them in order is not so simple as it
may seem. Here are four of the most common flaws in narrative paragraphs, against which you may check your own first drafts:

I. INSUFFICIENT DETAIL. A few words, of course, can tell what
happened: "I saw an accident." But if the reader is to feel the whole
sequence of the experience, he needs details, and many of them. He
also needs in the first sentence or two some orientation to the general
scene—a topic sentence of setting and mood. The following is the
opening of a narrative paragraph from an essay that has already
logically discussed its thesis that "haste makes waste." It is not a
bad beginning, but a few more details, as we shall see in a moment,
would help us know where we are, and at what time of day or night:

> The sky was very dark. People were walking quickly in all
> directions. . . .

II. DETAILS OUT OF ORDER. The writer of the dark-sky paragraph
went on in her next two sentences with additional detail:

> The sky was very dark. People were walking quickly in all
> directions. The trees were tossing and swaying about. The air felt
> heavy, and lightning flickered here and there behind the gray sky.

But, clearly, the further details are out of order. Although she has
said the trees were moving, the air seems to have remained still.
She eventually rearranged these details, but not before committing
another error.

III. COMMENTS BREAKING INTO THE NARRATIVE FLOW. Our dark-
sky student went on to intrude an editorializing comment, and a
clever one at that. But she would have been better off letting her

* From "Shooting an Elephant," in *Shooting an Elephant and Other Essays* by
George Orwell, copyright 1945, 1946, 1949, 1950 by Sonia Brownell Orwell. Reprinted
by permission of Harcourt Brace Jovanovich, Inc., and Martin Secker & Warburg
Limited.

details *imply* the moral of the story. Here is her paragraph, revised after conference, with the opening details of setting filled and re-arranged, but with the intruding comment, which she actually deleted, left in italics to illustrate the fault:

> One day, going home from school, I came to understand for the first time how costly haste can be. The sky was very dark, and people were walking quickly across the streets through the afternoon traffic. The air was heavy, and lightning flickered here and there behind the overcast. Suddenly a soft wind moved through the trees, setting them tossing and swaying; and then came a great gust, sending leaves and papers scurrying, and rattling shop signs. Wet splotches the size of quarters began to dapple the sidewalk; and then it started to pour. Everyone began to run in a frenzied scramble for shelter. *People should not lose their heads at the very time they need them most.* At the street corner ahead of me, two girls, running from different directions, crashed together. A boy riding a bicycle slammed on his brakes to avoid them, and he went skidding, out of control, into the middle of the street. A car caught him squarely. Next day, still stunned, I read in the paper that he had died on the way to the hospital.

IV. SHIFTING VIEWPOINT. The effect of a shift of viewpoint is about the same as that of the intruding comment. The narrative flow is broken. The author seems to have jumped out of his original assumptions, from one location to another, as the italicized sentence shows:

> My boys of Tent Five were suddenly all piling on top of me on the shaky bunk. I didn't feel much like a counselor, but at least I was keeping them amused. The giggling heap on top of me seemed happy enough. It was organized recreation time, and they seemed pretty well organized. *The Chief hurried across the camp ground, wondering what was going on over there, and issuing a silent death warrant for the counselor of Five.* I looked out through a wiggly chink in the heap and saw the Chief in the doorway, with his face growing redder and redder.

The writer of this paragraph has let his imagination shift from his recollected location on the bunk, beneath the heap of boys, to his reconstruction of what must have been going on in the Chief's head, out on the campground. Similar unwarranted shifts occur when you have been writing *he,* and suddenly shift to *they,* or when you unwittingly shift your tenses from present to past, or past to present.

EXPOSITORY PARAGRAPHS—DESCRIBING A PROCESS

Liven description with argument, with your own voice.

The most frequent use of speech—oral or written—is the giving of directions, that is, describing a process. "Turn left, go one block, turn right, go another block; eat at the Campbell House"—you have routed an inquirer to the nearest restaurant. If, instead, you have routed him to the nearest *good* restaurant, you have *offered an opinion* with your directions. Hence an argumentative edge—the speaker's voice—can liven the simplest description of a process, or what we might call simple exposition.

In 1653, Isaak Walton published *The Compleat Angler,* a delightful compendium of all he knew about fishing and cookery. In the following passage, Walton is doing something familiar: he is explaining what he thinks to be the best way of preparing and cooking a particular kind of fish, the chub. In other words, he is offering his opinion *and* explaining a simple process.

> The Chub, though he eat well thus dressed, yet as he is usually dressed he does not: he is objected against, not only for being full of small forked bones, dispersed through all his body, but that he eats waterish, and that the flesh of him is not firm, but short and tasteless. The French esteem him so mean, as to call him *un Vilain;* nevertheless he may be so dressed as to make him very good meat: as, namely, if he be a large Chub, then dress him thus:—
>
> First scale him, and then wash him clean, and then take out his guts; and to that end make the hole as little and near to his gills as you may conveniently, and especially make clean his throat from the grass and weeds that are usually in it, for if that be not very clean, it will make him to taste very sour. Having so done, put some sweet herbs into his belly; and then tie him with two or three splinters to a spit, and roast him, basted often with vinegar, or rather verjuice and butter, with good store of salt mixed with it.
>
> Being thus dressed, you will find him a much better dish of meat than you or most folk, even than Anglers themselves, do imagine; for this dries up the fluid watery humor with which all Chubs do abound.
>
> But take this rule with you, that a Chub newly taken and newly dressed is so much better than a Chub of a day's keeping after he is dead, that I can compare him to nothing so fitly as to cherries newly gathered from a tree, and others that have been bruised and lain a day or two in water. But the Chub being thus used and dressed presently, and not washed after he is gutted,—for note, that, lying long in water, and washing the blood out of any fish

after they be gutted, abates much of their sweetness, — you will find the Chub, being dressed in the blood and quickly, to be such meat as will recompense your labor and disabuse your opinion.*

This passage goes far beyond straight exposition, precise as its directions are. For example, the first sentence, "The Chub, though he eat well thus dressed . . . short and tasteless," has Walton's mark on it. He often deliberately unbalances parallel sentences to advance an argument. Here, he would have a nice parallelism, ". . . though he eat well thus dressed, yet as he is usually dressed he does not. . . ." But he deliberately breaks the parallelism by adding over thirty words to one side, as if he were loading a seesaw to his advantage.

Although you may not be able to describe and identify all of Walton's rhetorical flourishes from three centuries ago, you should realize how much of his prose would be lost if one were to strip it of its argumentative edge, indeed of its personality. The same rule applies to your own work: each word, each phrase, you put on a page is not just a means for moving information; it is a piece of your personality written into reason.

* Izaak Walton and Charles Cotton, *The Compleat Angler, or The Contemplative Man's Recreation,* ed. James Russell Lowell (Boston: Little, Brown, and Company, 1889), pp. 66–67.

EXERCISES

1 Write a paragraph describing a unit of space, taking your reader from the outside to the inside of your own home, for instance, or dealing with some interesting spatial unit as in the following paragraph from a student's paper.

The courtyard of the hotel at Uxmal was a wonderfully cool and welcome surprise after the sweaty bus trip out from Mérida. Surrounding the whole yard was a large *galería,* its ceiling blocking out the few rays of the sun that managed to filter through the heavy plantings that filled the yard. Overhead, along the *galería,* ceiling fans quietly turned, and underfoot the glazed tile floors felt smooth and delightfully cool even though the temperature on the road had pushed up past 100 degrees. Airy wicker chairs lined the railing, and just a few feet away, flowering jungle plants rose almost to the top of the stone arches on the second floor. Under the branches of a tall tree in the middle of the courtyard, out beyond the rail and the thick plantings, raised tile walkways crisscrossed the yard, bordered all along by neatly cultivated jungle flowers. And right in the middle of the yard, at the base of the big tree, a small waterfall splashed down over mossy rocks into a tiny bathing pool. The splashing water, the shade, the cool tile, all made the road outside seem very far off indeed.

2 Write a one-paragraph description of a person, blending space and time, as in the paragraph on Colonel Prynne (p. 29), including details of appearance, as well as surroundings.

3 Write a paragraph in which you blend the incidents and thoughts of a crucial moment, as in Orwell's paragraph on pp. 30–31.

4 Write two paragraphs that would be part of a longer essay, using the following excerpt from Alfred Kazin's *Starting Out in the Thirties* as a model (notice the effective topic sentence in both paragraphs).

The dinner was not a success. I kept trying to see everything through Ferguson's eyes, and I felt that everything looked very strange to him. For the first time, I had brought into our home someone from "outside," from the great literary world, and as Ferguson patiently smiled away, interrupted only by my mother's bringing in more and more platters and pleading with him to *eat something*, I tried to imagine his reactions. We all sat around him at the old round table in the dining room — my father, my little sister, and myself — and there poor Ferguson, his eyes bulging with the strain and the harsh bright lights from the overhead lamp, his cheeks red with effort, kept getting shoveled into him cabbage and meatballs, chicken, meat loaf, endless helpings of seltzer and cherry soda; and all the while I desperately kept up a line of chatter to show him that he was not completely isolated, our cousin Sophie sat at the table silently staring at him, taking him in. In our boxlike rooms, where you could hear every creak, every cough, every whisper, while the Brooklyn street boiled outside, there was a strangled human emotion that seemed to me unworthy of Ferguson's sophistication, his jazz, his sardonic perch on Union Square. But as Sophie sat at the table in her withdrawn silence, my sister stared wide-eyed at the visitor, my mother bustlingly brought in more platters, and my father explained that he had always followed and admired the *New Republic* — oh, ever since the days of Walter Lippmann and Herbert Croly! — I felt, through Ferguson's razor-sharp eyes, how dreary everything was. My father kept slurping the soup and reaching out for the meat with his own fork; since I had warned him that Ferguson would expect a drink, he self-consciously left the bottle of whiskey on the table and kept urging our visitor all through the meal to take another drink. My mother, who did not have even her personal appreciation of the *New Republic* to regale Ferguson with, had nothing to do but bring food in, and after a while Sophie took to her room and barricaded herself in.

So the meal which I had so much advertised in advance — which I had allowed Ferguson to believe would be exotic, mysterious, vaguely Levantine — passed at last, and after he had charmingly said good-by to my parents and I walked him back to the subway at Rockaway Avenue, he studied me quietly for a moment and said, "What the hell was so exotic about that?" . . .*

* Boston: Little, Brown and Company, 1965, pp. 45–57. Copyright © 1962, 1965 by Alfred Kazin. By permission of Little, Brown and Co. in association with The Atlantic Monthly Press.

5 **a.** Using the flattest, the most expressionless, the sparest of contemporary English, reduce the passage from Walton's *The Compleat Angler* to the bare skeleton of its information. Try to eliminate Walton entirely, leaving behind only a mechanical account of the information he imparted.

b. Having murdered Walton's prose, now try your hand at resurrecting it, but this time use *your own voice*. Rearrange the passage, reword it, reshape it any way you want, but preserve the skeletal framework of information you found in both the original and in your stripped version. In short, make the prose your own.

6 Write a five-hundred-word description of a process you know well — how to organize a demonstration, how to make a bracelet, a candle, a belt, a cake, how an internal combustion engine works. This is straight exposition. It will introduce you to the fine dry air of objectivity; to the problem of laying out in orderly sequence, for the reader's gathering comprehension, details that are in fact simultaneous; and to the difficulty of finding the clear, accurate, and descriptive phrase.

7 Now find a thesis that will change this description into an argument making some statement *about* the subject: organizing a demonstration requires a head for detail; making a cake is no child's play; what's under the hood is really no mystery. Rewrite the first paper using your new thesis and using, in some way, everything you said before.

Five
Evidence

Now with the whole essay in hand, we need just a little more thought. We need to check the evidence. Have you brought in enough to prove your point? Have you bored your reader with too much? Where can it go wrong? And what is evidence anyway?

Use specific examples.

Evidence is simply an example, something specific to illustrate your general thesis. And your thesis itself will suggest what examples you need. If you are supporting the thesis "Welfare breeds irresponsibility," describe several irresponsible welfare recipients—some you know. To illustrate that a character in a novel is unbelievable, describe the inconsistencies you noticed in him when you read it. Your thesis, your big idea, will emerge from the specific things you have seen, in person, in print, or on TV. Now use these things to support your thesis in turn. Make them brief, but sufficient. Three, proverbially, is an ideal number. But remember also that one extended description—a lonely old neighbor, an abandoned building, a high-speed scrape with automotive death—gives extremely interesting and persuasive evidence, especially when introduced with two or three brief examples, a statistic from the paper, a quotation from *Time,* an observation from yesterday morning.

Several examples are always better than one. One, all alone, implies a universality it may not have. It raises the nagging problem you have already worked at in developing your thesis and its contraries: the problem of unexamined assumptions, which lies behind all fallacies in logic, the mistake of assuming inadvertently that *one*, or *some*, equals *all*.

Check your assumptions.

Ask yourself, again, if your essay hangs on some unsuspected assumption. Suppose you have said that football builds character. As evidence, you have told how going out for practice has transformed a happy-go-lucky youth into a disciplined man with a part-time job and good grades. But you have assumed, without thinking, that nothing else would have worked as well, that football would work every time, that character consists only in self-discipline, and perhaps that women have no character at all. Your evidence is persuasive, but the hidden assumptions need resurfacing.

First, limit your assumptions by narrowing your thesis:

> **Although no magical guarantee, football strengthens the rugged and disciplined side of character.**

You then concede that some football players are downright wild, and that character includes social responsibility, moral courage, intelligence, compassion. (You can then probably claim some of these back for football too.) Then bring in some more examples. Three different young players, who have matured in different ways, would strengthen your point, and would assume only reasonable virtues for pigskin and practice.

Try an occasional definition.

Definitions are also a kind of conjectural filling out of the evidence. They can be stiff, especially straight from the dictionary, and they frequently over-explain what your words and evidence have already made clear. Nevertheless, they can clarify some concept you believe in, like "conservation," say, or "Women's Lib," by analyzing it into its parts, with examples for each, by bringing in contrasts and analogies, saying what it is like and what it is not like, as Stokely Carmichael does in explaining "Black Power":

> **Black Power means, for example, that in Lowndes County, Alabama, a black sheriff can end police brutality. A black tax assessor and tax collector and county board of revenue can lay, collect, and channel tax monies for the building of better roads and schools serving black people. In such areas as Lowndes, where black people have a majority, they will attempt to use power to exercise control. This is what they seek: control. When black people lack a majority, Black Power means proper representation and sharing**

of control. It means the creation of power bases, of strength, from which black people can press to change local or nation-wide patterns of oppression—instead of from weakness.

It does not mean *merely* putting black faces into office. Black visibility is not Black Power. Most of the black politicians around the country today are not examples of Black Power. The power must be that of a community, and emanate from there. The black politicians must start from there. The black politicians must stop being representatives of "downtown" machines, whatever the cost might be in terms of lost patronage and holiday handouts.*

Check your authorities.

I have just augmented my own evidence by quoting an authority. Authorities are impressive. We reasonably assume that they are right. What they say—about population, pollution, economics, tooth decay—is indeed most persuasive evidence. Use them. Quote them directly, if you can, and put your source in a footnote (see pp. 96–99):

> According to Sigmund Freud, establishing the ego is a kind of "reclamation work, like the draining of the Zuyder Zee."[1]

> [1] *New Introductory Lectures on Psycho-Analysis,* trans. W. J. H. Sprott (New York: W. W. Norton & Co., 1933), p. 112.
>> [I omit the author's name in the footnote because I have already named him in my text. I have quoted the shortest possible segment of Freud's sentence to get the sharpest focus, and I have run it into my own sentence within quotation marks. You would indent and single-space a long quotation, and omit the quotation marks: for further details see p. 96.]

An indirect reference, footnoted, works as well:

> Freud likens psychotherapy to reclaiming territory from the sea.[1]

The mere name of a Freud, an Einstein, or a Shakespeare can touch your paper with power.

But citing an authority risks four common fallacies. The first is in appealing to the authority outside of his field, even if his field is the universe. Although Einstein was a man of powerful intellect, we should not assume he knew all about economics too. The second fallacy is in misrepresenting what the authority really says. Sir Arthur Eddington (I cite another authority) puts the case: "It is a common mistake to suppose that Einstein's theory of relativity asserts that everything is relative. Actually it says, 'There are absolute things

* Stokely Carmichael and Charles V. Hamilton, *Black Power, the Politics of Liberation in America* (New York: Random House, 1967), p. 15.

in the world but you must look deeply for them. The things that first present themselves to your notice are for the most part relative.' "*
If you appeal loosely to Einstein to show that "everything is relative," you have misrepresented his theory. The third fallacy is in assuming that one instance from an authority represents him accurately. In one place, Shakespeare calls women fiends; in another, angels. The fourth fallacy is deepest: the authority may have faded. New facts have generated new ideas. Einstein has limited Newton's authority. Geology and radioactive carbon have challenged the authority of Genesis. Jung has challenged Freud; and Keynes, Marx. So ask these four questions:

1. Am I citing this authority outside his field?
2. Am I presenting him accurately?
3. Is this instance really representative?
4. Is he still fully authoritative?

Do not claim too much for him, and add other kinds of proof, preferably an example you yourself have seen. In short, don't put all your aids in one basket.

Check your conclusions.

What you conclude from your evidence is equally open to question. So question yourself, before your final draft. Put your faith in probability. If you say, "Apples are good food," you assume boldly that *all* apples are good, and you are not upset by the bad one in the barrel. You know that bad apples are neither so numerous nor so typical that you must conclude, "Apples are unfit for human consumption." You also know what causes the bad ones. So see that probability supports your generalization by checking the following conditions:

1. Your samples are reasonably numerous.
2. Your samples are truly typical.
3. Your exceptions are explainable, and demonstrably not typical.

Question your statistics. They can deceive badly because they look so solid—especially averages and percentages. "The average student earns ten dollars a week" may conceal the truth that one earns a hundred dollars and nine earn nothing. And a sample of ten students hardly represents thirty thousand. Moreover, each "one" in any statistical count represents a slightly different quantity, as a

* *The Nature of the Physical World* (Ann Arbor: University of Michigan Press, 1958), p. 23.

glance around a class of twenty students makes clear. So use your statistics with understanding, preferably with other specific examples.

Then, finally, ask if your evidence might not support some other conclusion. Some linguists, for example, have concluded that speech is superior to writing because speech has more "signals" than writing. But from the same evidence one might declare speech inferior: writing conveys the same message with fewer signals.

In the end, your evidence depends on common sense. Don't assume that one swallow makes a summer, and also check your generalizations for the following fallacies:

1. EITHER-OR. You assume only two opposing possibilities: "either we abolish requirements or education is finished." Education will probably amble on, somewhere in between.

2. OVERSIMPLIFICATION. As with *either-or,* you ignore alternatives. "A student learns only what he wants to learn" ignores all the pressures from parents and society, which in fact account for a good deal of learning.

3. BEGGING THE QUESTION. A somewhat unhandy term, which we have already seen (p. 5): you assume as proved something that really needs proving. "Free all political prisoners" assumes that none of those concerned has committed an actual crime.

4. IGNORING THE QUESTION. The question of whether it is right for a neighborhood to organize against a newcomer shifts to land values and taxes.

5. NON SEQUITUR. ("It does not follow.") "He's certainly sincere; he must be right." "He's the most popular; he should be president." The conclusions do not reasonably follow from sincerity and popularity.

6. POST HOC, ERGO PROPTER HOC. ("After this, therefore because of this.") The non sequitur of events: "He stayed up late and therefore won the race." He probably won in spite of late hours, and for other reasons.

7. FALSE ANALOGY. "You should choose your wife as you would your car." A person is not a machine, so that the analogy is unacceptable.

EXERCISES

1 After each of the following assertions, write two or three short questions that will challenge its assumptions, questions like "Good for what? Throwing? Fertilizer?" For example: Girls are brighter than boys. "At what age? In chess? In physics?"

    1. Men are superior to women.

    2. The backfield made some mistakes.

    3. Communism means violent repression.

    4. Don't trust anyone over thirty.

    5. All men are equal.

    6. The big companies are ruining the environment.

    7. Travel is educational.

    8. Our brand is free of tar.

    9. The right will prevail.

    10. A long walk is good for you.

2 Try a definition of a term like "barometer," "computer," "class," "humanities," "intelligence." Avoid the scent of the dictionary. If you try a larger term, break it down into parts. And establish firm boundaries for your term by considering what it is like, not like; what it does, does not do; what it is, is not.

3 Each of the following statements contains at least one fallacious citation of authority. Identify it, and explain how it involves one or several of these reasons: "Outside Field," "Not Accurately Presented," "Not Representative," "Out of Date."

    1. According to Charles Morton, a distinguished eighteenth-century theologian and schoolmaster, the swallows of England disappear to the dark side of the moon in winter.

    2. Einstein states that everything is relative.

    3. "Nucular" is an acceptable pronunciation of "nuclear." President Eisenhower himself pronounced it this way.

    4. War between capitalists and communists is inevitable, as Karl Marx shows.

    5. Giving LSD to everyone, including children, as Timothy Leary says, will greatly improve modern society.

    6. The American economy should be controlled in every detail; after all, economist John Kenneth Galbraith comes out for control.

    7. "Smooths are America's finest cigarette," says Joe Namath.

4 Name and explain the fallacy in each of the following:

1. Jones is rich. He must be dishonest.

2. He either worked hard for his money, or he is just plain lucky.

3. The best things in life are free, like free love.

4. Sunshine breeds flies, because when the sun shines the flies come out.

5. If they have no bread, let them eat cake. Cake is both tastier and richer in calories.

6. This is another example of American imperialism.

7. Smith's canned-soup empire reaches farther than the Roman empire.

8. *Chips* is America's most popular soap. It is clearly the best.

9. The draft is illegal. It takes young men away from their education and careers at the most crucial period of their lives. They lose thousands of dollars' worth of their time.

10. Women are the most exploited people in the history of the world.

11. Two minutes after the accused left the building, the bomb exploded.

12. The human mind is only an elaborate computer, because both can do complex calculations and make decisions.

Six
Writing Good Sentences

All this time you have been writing sentences, as naturally as breathing, and perhaps with as little variation. Now for a close look at the varieties of the sentence. Some varieties can be shaggy and tangled indeed. But they are all offshoots of the simple active sentence, the basic English genus *John hits Joe,* with action moving straight from subject through verb to object.

This subject-verb-object sentence can be infinitely grafted and contorted, but there are really only two general varieties of it: (1) the "loose, or strung-along," in Aristotle's phrase, and (2) the periodic. English naturally runs "loose." Our thoughts are by nature strung along from subject through verb to object, with whatever comes to mind simply added as it comes. The loose sentence puts its subject and verb early. But we can also use the periodic sentence characteristic of our Latin and Germanic ancestry, where ideas hang in the air like girders until all interconnections are locked by the final word, at the period: *John, the best student in the class, the tallest and most handsome, hits Joe.* A periodic sentence, in other words, is one that suspends its meaning until the end, usually with subject and verb widely separated, and the verb as near the end as possible.

So we have two varieties of the English sentence. The piece-by-piece and the periodic species simply represent two ways of thought: the first, the natural stringing of thoughts as they come; the second, the more careful contrivance of emphasis and suspense.

THE SIMPLE SENTENCE

Use the simple active sentence, loosely periodic.
Your best sentences will be hybrids of the loose and the periodic. First, learn to use active verbs (*John* HITS *Joe*), which will keep you within the simple active pattern with all parts showing (subject-verb-object), as opposed to a verb in the passive voice (*Joe* IS HIT *by John*), which puts everything backwards and uses more words. Then learn to give your native strung-along sentence a touch of periodicity and suspense.

Any change in normal order can give you unusual emphasis, as when you move the object ahead of the subject:

> **That I like.**
> **The house itself she hated, but the yard was grand.**
> **Nature I loved; and next to Nature, Art.**

Most times, we expect our ideas one at a time, in normal succession—*John hits Joe*—and with anything further added, in proper sequence, at the end—*a real haymaker.* Change this fixed way of thinking, and you immediately put your reader on the alert for something unusual. Consequently, some of your best sentences will be simple active ones sprung wide with phrases coloring subject, verb, object, or all three, in various ways. You may, for instance, effectively complicate the subject:

> **King Lear, proud, old, and childish, probably aware that his grip on the kingdom is beginning to slip, devises a foolish plan.**

Or the verb:

> **A good speech usually begins quietly, proceeds sensibly, gathers momentum, and finally moves even the most indifferent audience.**

Or the object:

> **Her notebooks contain marvelous comments on the turtle in the back yard, the flowers and weeds, the great elm by the drive, the road, the earth, the stars, and the men and women of the village.**

COMPOUND AND COMPLEX SENTENCES

Learn the difference between compound and complex sentences.
You make a compound sentence by linking together simple sentences with a coordinating conjunction (*and, but, or, nor, for, so*) or

with a colon or a semicolon. You make a complex one by hooking lesser sentences onto the main sentence with *that, which, who,* or one of the many other subordinating connectives like *although, because, where, when, after, if.* The compound sentence *coordinates,* treating everything on the same level; the complex *subordinates,* putting everything else somewhere below its one main self-sufficient idea. The compound links ideas one after the other, as in the basic simple sentence; the complex is a simple sentence elaborated by clauses instead of merely by phrases. The compound represents the strung-along way of thinking; the complex frequently represents the periodic.

Avoid simple-minded compounds.

Essentially the compound sentence *is* simple-minded, a set of clauses on a string—a child's description of a birthday party, for instance: "We got paper hats and we pinned the tail on the donkey and we had chocolate ice cream and Randy sat on a piece of cake and I won third prize." *And . . . and . . . and.*

But this way of thinking is always useful for pacing off related thoughts, and for breaking the staccato of simple statement. It often briskly connects cause and effect: "The clock struck one, and down he run." "The solipsist relates all knowledge to his own being, and the demonstrable commonwealth of human nature dissolves before his dogged timidity." The compound sentence is built on the most enduring of colloquial patterns—the simple sequence of things said as they occur to the mind—it has the pace, the immediacy, and the dramatic effect of talk. Hemingway, for instance, often gets all the numb tension of a shell-shocked mind by reducing his character's thoughts all to one level, in sentences something like this: "It was a good night and I sat at a table and . . . and . . . and . . . ."

Think of the compound sentence in terms of its conjunctions—the words that yoke its clauses—and of the accompanying punctuation. Here are three basic groups of conjunctions that will help you sort out and punctuate your compound thoughts.

GROUP I. *The three common coordinating conjunctions:* and, but, *and* or (nor). *Put a comma before each.*

I like her, and I don't mind saying so.
Art is long, but life is short.
Win this point, or the game is lost.

GROUP II. *Conjunctive adverbs:* therefore, moreover, however, nevertheless, consequently, furthermore. *Put a semicolon before, and a comma after each.*

Nations indeed seem to have a kind of biological span like human life, from rebellious youth, through caution, to decay; consequently, predictions of doom are not uncommon.

GROUP III. *Some in-betweeners*—yet, still, so—*which sometimes take a comma, sometimes a semicolon, depending on your pace and emphasis.*

We long for the good old days, yet we never include the disadvantages.
People long for the good old days; yet they rarely take into account the inaccuracy of human memory.
The preparation had been halfhearted and hasty, so the meeting was wretched.
Rome declined into the pleasures of its circuses and couches; so the tough barbarians conquered.

Try compounding without conjunctions.
Though the conjunction usually governs its compound sentence, two powerful coordinators remain—the semicolon and the colon alone. For contrasts, the semicolon is the prince of coordinators.

The dress accents the feminine; the pants suit speaks for freedom.
Golf demands the best of time and space; tennis, the best of personal energy.
The government tries to get the most out of taxes; the individual tries to get out of the most taxes.

The colon similarly pulls two "sentences" together without blessing of conjunction, period, or capital. But it signals amplification, not contrast: the second clause explains the first.

A house with an aging furnace costs more than the asking price suggests: ten dollars more a month in fuel means about eighty dollars more a year.
A growing population means more business: more business will exhaust our supply of ores in less than half a century.
Sports at any age are beneficial: they keep your pulses hopping.

Learn to subordinate.
You probably write compound sentences almost without thinking. But the subordinations of the complex usually require some thought. Indeed, you are ranking closely related thoughts, arranging the lesser ones so that they bear effectively on your main thought. You must first pick your most important idea. You must then change mere sequence into subordination—ordering your lesser thoughts

"sub," or below, the main idea. The childish birthday sentence, then, might come out something like this:

> After we got paper hats and ate chocolate ice cream, after Randy sat on a piece of cake and everyone pinned the tail on the donkey, I WON THIRD PRIZE.

You do the trick with connectives — with any word, like *after* in the sentence above, indicating time, place, cause, or other qualification. Now something more ambitious:

> *If* they try, *if* they fail, THEY ARE STILL GREAT *because* their spirit is unbeaten.

You daily achieve subtler levels of subordination with the three relative pronouns *that, which, who,* and with the conjunction *that. That, which,* and *who* connect thoughts so closely related as to seem almost equal, but actually each tucks a clause (subject-and-verb) into some larger idea:

> The car, *which* runs perfectly, is not worth selling.
> The car *that* runs perfectly is worth keeping.
> He thought *that* the car would run forever.
> He thought [*that* omitted but understood] the car would run forever.

But the subordinating conjunctions and adverbs (*although, if, because, since, until, where, when, as if, so that*) really put subordinates in their places. Look at *when* in this sentence of E. B. White's from *Charlotte's Web:*

> Next morning *when* the first light came into the sky and the sparrows stirred in the trees, *when* the cows rattled their chains and the rooster crowed and the early automobiles went whispering along the road, Wilbur awoke and looked for Charlotte.

Here the simple *when,* used only twice, has regimented five subordinate clauses, all of equal rank, into their proper station below that of the main clause, "Wilbur awoke and looked for Charlotte." You can vary the ranking intricately and still keep it straight:

> *Although* some claim *that* time is an illusion, *because* we have no absolute chronometer, *although* the mind cannot effectively grasp time, *because* the mind itself is a kind of timeless presence almost oblivious to seconds and hours, *although* the time of our solar system may be only an instant in the universe at large, WE STILL CAN-

NOT QUITE DENY *that* some progression of universal time is passing over us, *if* only we could measure it.

Complex sentences are, at their best, really simple sentences gloriously delayed and elaborated with subordinate thoughts. The following beautiful and elaborate sentence from the Book of Common Prayer is all built on the simple sentence "draw near":

Ye who do truly and earnestly repent you of your sins, and are in love and charity with your neighbors, and intend to lead a new life, following the commandments of God, and walking from henceforth in his holy ways, draw near with faith, and take this holy sacrament to your comfort, and make your humble confession to Almighty God, devoutly kneeling.

Even a short sentence may be complex, attaining a remarkably varied suspense. Notice how the simple statement "I allowed myself" is skillfully elaborated in this sentence by the late Wolcott Gibbs of *The New Yorker:*

Twice in my life, for reasons that escape me now, though I'm sure they were discreditable, I allowed myself to be persuaded that I ought to take a hand in turning out a musical comedy.

Try for still closer connections: modify.
Your subordinating *if's* and *when's* have really been modifying — that is, limiting — the things you have attached them to. But there is a smoother way. It is an adjectival sort of thing, a shoulder-to-shoulder operation, a neat trick with no need for shouting, a stone to a stone with no need for mortar. You simply put clauses and phrases up against a noun, instead of attaching them with a subordinator. This sort of modification includes the following constructions, all using the same close masonry: (1) appositives, (2) relatives understood, (3) adjectives-with-phrase, (4) participles, (5) absolutes.

APPOSITIVES. Those phrases about shoulders and tricks and stones, above, are all in apposition with *sort of thing,* and they are grammatically subordinate to it. The phrases are nevertheless nearly coordinate and interchangeable. They are compressions of a series of sentences ("It is an adjectival sort of thing. It is a neat trick . . . ," and so forth) set side by side, "stone to stone." Mere contact does the work of the verb *is* and its subject *it.* English often does the same with subordinate clauses, omitting the *who is* or *which is* and putting the rest directly into apposition. "The William who is the Conqueror" becomes "William the Conqueror." "The Jack who is

the heavy hitter" becomes "Jack the heavy hitter." These, incidentally, are called "restrictive" appositions, because they restrict to a
particular designation the nouns they modify, setting this William
and this Jack apart from all others (with no separating commas).
Similarly, you can make nonrestrictive appositives from nonrestrictive clauses, clauses that simply add information (between commas).
"Smith, who is a man to be reckoned with, . . ." becomes "Smith, a
man to be reckoned with, ..." "Jones, who is our man in Liverpool,
. . ." becomes "Jones, our man in Liverpool, ..." Restrictive or
nonrestrictive, close contact makes your point with economy and
fitness.

RELATIVES UNDERSTOOD. You can often achieve the same economy, as I have already hinted, by omitting any kind of relative and
its verb, thus gaining a compression both colloquial and classic:

> A comprehension [that is] both colloquial and classic . . . .
> The specimens [that] he had collected . . . .
> The girl [whom] he [had] left behind . . . .

ADJECTIVES-WITH-PHRASE. This construction is also appositive
and adjectival. It is neat and useful:

> The law was passed, *thick with provisions and codicils, heavy with
> implications.*
> There was the lake, *smooth in the early-morning air.*

PARTICIPLES. Participles—verbs acting as adjectives—are extremely supple subordinators. Consider this sequence of six simple
sentences:

> He had been thrown.
> He had accepted.
> He felt a need.
> He demanded money.
> He failed.
> He chose not to struggle.

Now see how Richard Wright, in *Native Son*, subordinates the first
five of these to the sixth with participles. He elaborates the complete thought into a forceful sentence that runs for eighty-nine words
with perfect clarity:

> *Having been thrown* by an accidental murder into a position where
> he had sensed a possible order and meaning in his relations with
> the people about him; *having accepted* the moral guilt and respon-
> sibility for that murder because it had made him feel free for the

first time in his life; *having felt* in his heart some obscure need to be at home with people and *having demanded* ransom money to enable him to do it—*having* done all this and *failed,* he chose not to struggle any more.

These participles have the same adjectival force:

Dead to the world, *wrapped* in sweet dreams, *untroubled* by bills, he slept till noon.

Notice that the participles operate exactly as the adjective *dead* does.

Beware of dangling participles. They may trip you, as they have tripped others. The participle, with its adjectival urge, may grab the first noun that comes along, with shocking results:

Bowing to the crowd, the bull caught him unawares.
Observing quietly from the bank, the beavers made several errors in judgment.
Squandering everything at the track, the money was never repaid.
What we need is a list of teachers broken down alphabetically.

Move the participle next to its intended noun or pronoun; you will have to supply this word if inadvertence or the passive voice has omitted it entirely. Recast the sentence for good alignment when necessary. You may also save the day by changing a present participle to a past, as in the third example below.

The bull caught him unawares as he bowed to the crowd.
Observing quietly from the bank, they saw the beavers make several errors in judgment.
Squandered at the track, the money was never repaid.
What we need is an alphabetical list of teachers.

ABSOLUTES. The absolute phrase has a great potential of polished economy. Many an absolute is simply a prepositional phrase with the preposition dropped:

He ran up the stairs, [with] *a bouquet of roses under his arm,* and rang the bell.
She walked slowly, [with] *her camera ready.*

But the ablative absolute (*ablative* means "removed") is removed from the main clause, borrowing tense and modifying only by proximity. If you have had some Latin, you will probably remember this construction as some kind of brusque condensation, something like *"The road completed,* Caesar moved his camp." But it survives in the best of circles. Somewhere E. B. White admits to feeling particularly good one morning, just having brought off an especially fine ablative absolute. And it is actually more common than you may suppose. A recent newspaper article stated that "the Prince has fled the country, *his hopes of a negotiated peace shattered.*" The *hopes shattered* pattern (noun plus participle) marks the ablative absolute (also called, because of the noun, a "nominative absolute"). The idea might have been more conventionally subordinated: "since his hopes were shattered" or "with his hopes shattered." But the ablative absolute accomplishes the subordination with economy and style.

Take a regular subordinate clause: "*When* the road *was* completed." Cut the subordinator and reduce the verb. You now have an ablative absolute, a phrase that stands absolutely alone, shorn of both its connective *when* and its full predication *was: "The road completed,* Caesar moved his camp." Basically a noun and a participle, or noun and adjective, it is a kind of grammatical shorthand, a telegram: *ROAD COMPLETED CAESAR MOVED* — most said in fewest words, speed with high compression. This is its appeal and its power.

> **The cat stopped,** *its back arched, its eyes frantic.*
> **The whole economy,** *God willing,* **soon will return to normal.**
> *All things considered,* **the plan would work.**

PARALLEL CONSTRUCTION

Use parallels to strengthen equivalent ideas.
No long complex sentence will hold up without parallel construction. Paralleling can be very simple. Any word will seek its own kind, noun to noun, adjective to adjective, infinitive to infinitive. The simplest series of things automatically runs parallel:

> **shoes and ships and sealing wax**
> **I came, I saw, I conquered**
> **to be or not to be**
> **a dull, dark, and soundless day**
> **mediocre work, cowardly work, disastrous work**

But they very easily run out of parallel too, and this you must learn to prevent. The last item especially may slip out of line, as in this series: "friendly, kind, unobtrusive, and *a bore*" (boring). The noun *bore* has jumped off the track laid by the preceding parallel adjectives. Your train of equivalent ideas should all be of the same grammatical kind to carry their equivalence clearly — to strengthen it: either parallel adjectives, *friendly, kind, unobtrusive,* and *boring,* or all nouns, *a friend, a saint, a diplomat,* and *a bore.* Your paralleling articles and prepositions should govern a series as a whole, or should accompany *every* item:

> a hat, cane, pair of gloves, and mustache
> a hat, a cane, a pair of gloves, and a mustache
> by land, sea, or air
> by land, by sea, or by air

Verbs also frequently intrude to throw a series of adjectives (or nouns) out of parallel:

> He thought the girl was *attractive, intelligent,* and *knew* how to make him feel needed.
> He thought the girl was *attractive, intelligent,* and *sympathetic,* knowing how to make him feel needed.

Watch the paralleling of pairs.

Pairs should be pairs, not odds and ends. Notice how the faulty pairs in these sentences have been corrected:

> She liked *the lawn and gardening* (the lawn and the garden).
> They were *all athletic or big men on campus* (athletes or big men on campus).
> They wanted *peace without being disgraced* (peace without dishonor).
> He was *shy but a creative boy* (shy but creative).

Check your terms on both sides of your coordinating conjunctions *(and, but, or)* and see that they match:

> Orientation week seems both worthwhile [adjective] and necessary
> a-necessity [noun].   that
> He prayed that they would leave and ∧ the telephone would not ring.

Learn to use paralleling coordinators.

The sentence above about "Orientation week" has used one of a number of useful (and tricky) parallel constructions: *both-and; either-or; not only-but also; not-but; first-second-third; as well as.* This last one is similar to *and,* a simple link between two equivalents, but it often causes trouble:

> One should take care of one's physical self [noun] *as well as* being [participle] able to read and write.

Again, the pair should be matched: "one's *physical self* as well as one's *intellectual self*," or "one's physical *self* as well as one's *ability* to read and write"—though this second is still slightly unbalanced, in rhetoric if not in grammar. The best cure would probably extend the underlying antithesis, the basic parallel:

> One should take care of one's physical self as well as one's intellectual self, of one's ability to survive as well as to read and write.

With the *either-or*'s and the *not only-but also*'s you continue the principle of pairing. The *either* and the *not only* are merely signposts of what is coming: two equivalents linked by a coordinating conjunction *(or* or *but)*. Beware of putting the signs in the wrong place —too soon for the turn.

He either is an absolute piker or a fool!

Neither in time nor space . . . .

He not only likes the girl but the family, too.

In these examples, the thought got ahead of itself, as in talk. Just make sure that the word following each of the two coordinators is of the same kind, preposition for preposition, article for article, adjective for adjective—for even with signs well placed, the parallel can skid:

> The students are not only organizing [present participle] social ac-
> discussing
> tivities, but also ~~are interested~~ [passive construction] ~~in~~ political questions.

Put identical parts in parallel places; fill in the blanks with the same parts of speech: "not only _____, but also _____." You similarly parallel the words following numerical coordinators:

> However variously he expressed himself, he unquestionably thought, first, *that* everyone could get ahead; second, *that* workers generally were paid more than they earned; and, third, *that* laws enforcing a minimum wage were positively undemocratic.
> For a number of reasons, he decided (1) that he did not like it, (2) that she would not like it, (3) that they would be better off without it. [Note that the parentheses around the numbers operate exactly as any parentheses, and need no additional punctuation.]
> My objections are obvious: (1) it is unnecessary, (2) it costs too much, and (3) it won't work.

In parallels of this kind, *that* is usually the problem, since you may easily, and properly, omit it when there is only one clause and no confusion:

> **. . . he unquestionably thought everyone could get ahead.**

If second and third clauses occur, as your thought moves along, you may have to go back and put up the first signpost:

> **that**
> **. . . he unquestionably thought** ∧ **everyone could get ahead, that**
> **workers . . . , and that laws . . . .**

Enough of *that*. Remember simply that equivalent thoughts demand parallel constructions. Notice the clear and massive strategy in the following sentence from the concluding chapter of Freud's last book, *An Outline of Psychoanalysis.* Freud is not only summing up the previous discussion, but also expressing the quintessence of his life's work. He is pulling everything together in a single sentence. Each of the parallel *which* clauses gathers up, in proper order, an entire chapter of his book (notice the parallel force in repeating *picture,* and the summarizing dash):

> **The picture of an ego which mediates between the id and the external world, which takes over the instinctual demands of the former in order to bring them to satisfaction, which perceives things in the latter and uses them as memories, which, intent upon its self-preservation, is on guard against excessive claims from both directions, and which is governed in all its decisions by the injunctions of a modified pleasure principle — this picture actually applies to the ego only up to the end of the first period of childhood, till about the age of five.**

Such precision is hard to match. This is what parallel thinking brings — balance and control and an eye for sentences that seem intellectual totalities, as if struck out all at once from the uncut rock. Francis Bacon's sentences can seem like this (notice how he drops the verb after establishing his pattern):

> **For a crowd is not company, and faces are but a gallery of pictures,**
> **and talk but a tinkling cymbal, where there is no love.**
> **Reading maketh a full man; conference a ready man; and writing**
> **an exact man.**

And the balance can run from sentence to sentence through an entire passage, controlled not only by connectives repeated in parallel, but by whole phrases and sentences so repeated, as in this passage by Macaulay:

> To sum up the whole: we should say that the aim of the Platonic philosophy was to exalt man into a god. The aim of the Baconian philosophy was to provide man with what he requires while he continues to be man. The aim of the Platonic philosophy was to raise us far above vulgar wants. The aim of the Baconian philosophy was to supply our vulgar wants. The former aim was noble; but the latter was attainable.

THE LONG AND SHORT OF IT

Your style will emerge once you can manage some length of sentence, some intricacy of subordination, some vigor of parallel, and some play of long against short, of amplitude against brevity. Try the very long sentence, and the very short. The best short sentences are meatiest:

> I think; therefore, I am.
> The mass of men lead lives of quiet desperation.
> The more selfish the man, the more anguished the failure.

Experiment with the fragment.
The fragment is close to conversation. It is the laconic reply, the pointed afterthought, the quiet exclamation, the telling question. Try to cut and place it clearly (usually at beginnings and ends of paragraphs) so as not to lead your reader to expect a full sentence, or to suspect a poor writer:

> But no more. No, not really.
> First, a look behind the scenes. Enough of that.

The fragment, of course, usually counts as an error. The reader expects a sentence and gets only a fragment of one: you leave him hanging in air, waiting for the second shoe to fall, or the voice to drop, with the thought completed, at the period. The *rhetorical* fragment—the effective and persuasive one—leaves him satisfied: *Of course*. The *grammatical* fragment leaves him unsatisfied: *When the vote was counted*. A question hangs in the air: *what* happened? who won? who got mad? But the point here about rhetorical fragments is to use their short, conversational staccato as one of your means to vary the rhythm of your long and longer sentences, playing long against short.

Develop a rhythm of long and short.

The conversational flow between long and short makes a passage move. Study the subordinations, the parallels, and the play of short and long in this elegant passage of Virginia Woolf's — after you have read it once for sheer enjoyment. She is writing of Lord Chesterfield's famous letters to Philip Stanhope, his illegitimate son:

> But while we amuse ourselves with this brilliant nobleman and his views on life we are aware, and the letters owe much of their fascination to this consciousness, of a dumb yet substantial figure on the farther side of the page. Philip Stanhope is always there. It is true that he says nothing, but we feel his presence in Dresden, in Berlin, in Paris, opening the letters and poring over them and looking dolefully at the thick packets which have been accumulating year after year since he was a child of seven. He had grown into a rather serious, rather stout, rather short young man. He had a taste for foreign politics. A little serious reading was rather to his liking. And by every post the letters came — urbane, polished, brilliant, imploring and commanding him to learn to dance, to learn to carve, to consider the management of his legs, and to seduce a lady of fashion. He did his best. He worked very hard in the school of the Graces, but their service was too exacting. He sat down halfway up the steep stairs which lead to the glittering hall with all the mirrors. He could not do it. He failed in the House of Commons; he subsided into some small post in Ratisbon; he died untimely. He left it to his widow to break the news which he had lacked the heart or the courage to tell his father — that he had been married all these years to a lady of low birth, who had borne him children.
>
> The Earl took the blow like a gentleman. His letter to his daughter-in-law is a model of urbanity. He began the education of his grandsons . . . .*

Those are some sentences to copy. We immediately feel the rhythmic play of periodic and loose, parallel and simple, long and short. Such orchestration takes years of practice, but you can always begin.

* *The Second Common Reader,* p. 81. Copyright, 1932, by Harcourt Brace Jovanovich, Inc.; renewed, 1960, by Leonard Woolf. Reprinted by permission of Harcourt Brace Jovanovich, Inc., the Author's Literary Estate and The Hogarth Press, Ltd.

EXERCISES

1 Give each of the following sentences a touch of periodicity (that is, suspense) by changing the normal word order, by adding interruptive words or phrases, or by complicating one of the three principal elements of the sentence: the subject, the verb, the object.

EXAMPLE.   She made her way along the smoldering roof.

Carefully at first, then confidently, then with reckless steps, she made her way along the peak of the smoldering roof.

1. Commune residents are often escapees from solidly middle-class families.

2. Old friends are often shocked and embarrassed when they meet after years of separation and find they now have little in common.

3. Some firemen began carrying guns when they were frightened by the chaos of the riots.

4. The bottleneck in education is that the teacher can listen and respond to no more than one student at a time.

5. The car wheezed to a stop.

2 Write six compound sentences, two with *and,* two with *but,* two with *or (nor).* Try to get as grand a feeling of consequence as possible with your *and*'s: "Empires fall, and the saints come marching in."

3 Write three compound sentences using conjunctive adverbs, on the pattern: "_____; therefore, _____." Punctuate carefully with semicolon and comma.

4 Write three compound sentences in which the link is the semicolon alone. Try for meaningful contrasts.

EXAMPLE.   The county wants the new expressway; the city wants to renew its streets.

5 Write three compound sentences in which the link is a colon. Try to make the second half of the compound explain the first.

EXAMPLE.   His game was ragged: he went into sand traps four times, and into the trees five.

6 Here are some pairs of sentences. Convert them into complex sentences, trying to use a variety of subordinators.

1. He couldn't go on. He was just too tired.

2. The crime commission recommended a number of such programs. Federal funds have been made available for putting them into operation.

3. We can probably never perfect the process beyond its present state. We should still try.

4. Most schools are just now starting courses in computers for freshmen. To evaluate those programs will take several years.

5. On small farms labor was not specialized. On medium farms, labor was partially specialized. But large farms carefully divided their workers into teams of specialists.

7 Streamline the following sentences by using appositives wherever you can.

1. The security guard, who must have been a very frightened man, fired point-blank into the crowd.

2. Professor Stanley, who is now associate vice-president and director of business operations, has been named a vice-president at the University of Nebraska.

3. The book, which has been a best seller for several months, will be made into a movie.

4. American social mores have undergone staggering changes since the early 1950's. These changes are so great in quality and number as to constitute a virtual revolution.

5. The Globe Theatre, which was immediately acclaimed the best designed and appointed playhouse in London, was completed in 1599.

8 Consolidate the following sentences, using adjectival phrases and absolutes rather than subordinate clauses.

1. The young girl cowered in the corner. There was pure terror in her eyes.

2. This construction is also appositional and adjectival. It is a neat trick for the beginning writer to remember.

3. Its deck was splintered and peeling. Its rigging was nearly all frayed and rotted. The boat obviously hadn't been cared for at all.

4. Griswell had neither eaten nor slept, and when he stumbled into the bar he was trembling with fatigue.

5. The ladder was sagging with his weight, and at last it collapsed.

9 Keeping an eye out for dangling participles, revise the following sentences by transforming as many verbs as reasonably possible into participles.

1. Apparently the boxer thought the bell had sounded. He dropped his guard, and he was immediately knocked out.

2. He settled in to a Bohemian life in the French quarter. He started publishing in all the appropriate little magazines. And at last he found himself presiding over a colony of artists and writers.

3. The prisoners were obviously angered by the news that no guards were fired. They felt cheated and betrayed. And so on August 4 they seized three guards as hostages to force the warden to reconsider.

4. Dalton Trumbo was blacklisted in Hollywood; he was vilified in the press; and he was forced to write scripts under an assumed name until nearly 1960.

5. The student-designed rocket functioned perfectly. It rose one hundred miles above the earth, flew for ten minutes, traveled some fifty miles down range, and splashed down precisely on target.

10 Try turning the phrases and subordinate clauses in the following sentences into absolutes.

1. With examinations coming and with the temperature dropping, students are beginning to show up at the health service with all sorts of nebulous ailments, most of them purely imagined.

2. Ted left the room, leaving his things still scattered over the floor.

3. Even though the tank was filled with gas and the ignition was working perfectly, the engine still wouldn't start.

4. Even though the stock market had collapsed, and fifteen percent of the workers were jobless, Hoover nonetheless felt the economy would eventually right itself without tinkering.

5. When his three minutes were up, he deposited another quarter.

11 Correct the faulty parallelism in the following sentences from students' papers, and clean up any wordiness you find.

1. A student follows not only a special course of training, but among his studies and social activities finds a liberal education.

2. Either the critics attacked the book for its triteness, or it was criticized for its lack of organization.

3. This is not only the case with the young voters of the United States but also of the adult ones.

4. Certain things are not actually taught in the classroom. They are learning how to get along with others, to depend on oneself, and managing one's own affairs.

5. Knowing Greek and Roman antiquity is not just learning to speak their language but also their culture.

12 Write an imitation of the passage from Virginia Woolf on p. 57, choosing your own subject but matching the patterns, lengths, and rhythms of her sentences, sentence for sentence, if you can. At any rate, aim toward effective rhythms of long and short.

Seven
Correcting
Wordy
Sentences

Now let us contemplate evil—or at least the innocently awful, the bad habits that waste our words, fog our thoughts, and wreck our delivery. Our thoughts are naturally roundabout, our phrases naturally secondhand. Our satisfaction in merely getting something down on paper naturally blinds us to our errors and ineptitudes. It hypnotizes us into believing we have said what we meant, when our words actually say something else: "Every seat in the house was filled to capacity." Two ways of expressing one thought, two clichés, have collided: *every seat was taken* and *the house was filled to capacity*. Cut the excess wordage, and the absurd accident vanishes. Good sentences come from constant practice in correcting the bad.

Count your words.

Writing is devilish; the general sin is wordiness. We put down the first thought that comes, we miss the best order, and we then need lengths of *is*'s, *of*'s, *by*'s and *which*'s—words virtually meaning-less in themselves—to wire our meaningful words together again. Look for the two or three words that carry your meaning; then see if you can rearrange them to speak for themselves, cutting out all the little useless wirings:

This is the young man who was elected to be president by the class.
[The class elected this young man president. 7 words for 14]

Frequently you can reduce tautologies (p. 187):

61

each separate incident	each incident
many different ways	many ways
dash quickly	dash

As these examples show, the basic cure for wordiness is to count the words in any suspected sentence or phrase—and to make each word count. If you can rephrase to save even one word, your sentence will be clearer. And seek the active verb: *John* HITS *Joe.*

Shun the passive voice.

I have already mentioned the passive voice, and will return to it again (pp. 45; 129), but it is more wordy and deadly than most people imagine. It is also, alas, persistent.

> **It was voted that there would be a drive for the cleaning up of the people's park.** [*passive voice—17 words*]
> **We voted a drive to clean up the people's park.** [*active voice—10 words*]

The passive voice puts the cart before the horse: the object of the action first, then the harnessing verb, running backwards, then the driver forgotten, and the whole contraption at a standstill. The passive voice is simply "passive" action, the normal action backwards: object-verb-subject (with the true subject usually forgotten) instead of subject-verb-object—*Joe is hit by John* instead of *John hits Joe.*

The passive voice liquidates and buries the active individual, along with most of the awful truth. Our massed, scientific, and bureaucratic society is so addicted to it that you must constantly alert yourself against its drowsy, impersonal pomp. The simple English sentence is active; it *moves* from subject through verb to object: "The dean's office has turned down your proposal." But the impersonal bureau usually emits instead a passive smokescreen, and the student sees no one at all to help him:

> **It has been decided that your proposal for independent study is not sufficiently in line with the prescribed qualifications as outlined by the college in the catalog.**

Committees always write this way, and the effect on academic writing, as the professor goes from committee to desk to classroom, is astounding. "It was moved that a meeting would be held," the secretary writes, to avoid pinning the rap on anybody. So writes the professor, so writes the student.

I reluctantly admit that the passive voice has certain uses. In fact, your meaning sometimes demands the passive voice; the agent

may be better under cover—insignificant, or unknown, or mysterious. The active "Shrapnel hit him" seems to belie the uncanny
impersonality of "He was hit by shrapnel." The broad forces of history similarly demand the passive: "The West was opened in 1848."
Moreover, you may sometimes need the passive voice to place your
true subject, the hero of the piece, where you can modify him con-
veniently: *Joe was hit by John, who, in spite of all . . . .* And sometimes
it simply is more convenient: "This subject-verb-object sentence can
be infinitely contorted." You can, of course, find a number of passive constructions in this book, which preaches against them, because they can also space out a thought that comes too fast and thick.
In trying to describe periodic sentences, for instance (p. 44), I
changed "until all interconnections lock in the final word" (active)
to ". . . are locked by the final word" (passive). The *lock* seemed too
tight, especially with *in,* and the locking seemed contrary to the way
buildings *are built.* Yes, the passive has its uses.

But it is wordy. It puts useless words in a sentence. Its dullness
derives as much from its extra wordage as from its impersonality.
The best way to prune is with the active voice, cutting the passive
and its fungus as you go. Notice the effect on the following typical,
and actual, samples:

PASSIVE: Public concern *has* also *been given* a tremendous impetus
by the findings of the Hoover Commission on the federal government, and "little Hoover" commissions to survey the organizational structure and functions of many state governments *have
been established.*

ACTIVE: The findings of the Hoover Commission on federal government *have* also greatly stimulated public concern, and many
states *have established* "little Hoover" commissions to survey
their governments. [*27 words for 38*]

PASSIVE: The algal mats *are made up of* the interwoven filaments of
several genera.

ACTIVE: The interwoven filaments of several genera *make up* the
algal mats. [*11 words for 13*]

PASSIVE: Many of the remedies *would* probably *be shown to be* faith
cures.

ACTIVE: Many of the remedies *were* probably faith cures. [*8 words
for 12*]

PASSIVE: Anxiety and emotional conflict *are lessened* when latency
sets in. The total personality *is oriented* in a repressive, inhibitory
fashion so as to maintain the barriers, and what Freud has called
"psychic dams," against psychosexual impulses.

ACTIVE: **When latency sets in, anxiety and emotional conflict** *subside*. **The personality** *inhibits* **itself, maintaining its barriers —Freud's "psychic dams" — against psychosexual impulses.** [22 *words for 36*]

Check the stretchers.
To be, itself, frequently ought not to be:

He seems [to be] upset about something.
She considered him [to be] perfect.
This appears [to be] difficult.

Above all, keep your sentences awake by not putting them into those favorite stretchers of the passivists, *There is . . . which, It is . . . that,* and the like:

Moreover, [there is] one segment of the population [which] never seeks employment.
[There are] many women [who] never marry.
[There] is nothing wrong with it. [Nothing is . . . .]
[It is] his last book [that] shows his genius best.
[It is] this [that] is important.

Cut every *it* not referring to something. Next to activating your passive verbs, and cutting the passive *there is*'s and *it is*'s, perhaps nothing so improves your prose as to go through it systematically also deleting every *to be*, every *which, that, who,* and *whom* not needed for utter clarity or for spacing out a thought. All your sentences will feel better.

Beware the of-and-which disease.
The passive sentence frequently breaks out in a rash of *of*'s and *which*'s, and even the active sentence may suffer. Diagnosis: something like sleeping sickness. *With*'s, *in*'s, *to*'s, and *by*'s also inflamed. Surgery imperative. Here is an actual case:

Many biological journals, especially those *which* **regularly publish new scientific names, now state** *in* **each issue the exact date** *of* **publication** *of* **the preceding issue.** *In* **dealing** *with* **journals** *which* **do not follow this practice, or** *with* **volumes** *which* **are issued individually, the biologist often needs** *to* **resort** *to* **indexes . . .** *in order to* **determine the actual date** *of* **publication** *of* **a particular name.**

Note *of publication of* twice over, and the three *which*'s. The passage is a sleeping beauty. The longer you look at it, the more useless little attendants you see. Note the inevitable passive voice *(which are is-sued)* in spite of the author's active efforts. The *of*'s accompany extra nouns, *publication* repeating *publish,* for instance. Remedy: (1) eliminate *of*'s and their nouns, (2) change *which* clauses into participles, (3) change nouns into verbs. You can cut more than a third of this passage without touching the sense (using 39 words for 63):

> **Many biological journals, especially those regularly** *publishing* **new scientific names, now give the date of each preceding issue. With journals not** *following* **this practice, and with some books, the biologist must turn to indexes . . .** *to date* **a particular name.**

I repeat: you can cut most *which*'s, one way or another, with no loss of blood. Participles can modify their antecedents directly, since they are verbal adjectives, without an intervening *which:* "a car *which was* going south" is "a car going south"; "a train *which is* moving" is "a moving train." Similarly with the adjective itself: "a song *which was* popular last year" is "a song popular last year"; "a person *who is* attractive" is "an attractive person." Beware of this whole crowd: *who are, that was, which are.*

If you need a relative clause, remember *that. Which* has almost completely displaced it in labored writing. *That* is still best for restrictive clauses, those necessary to definition: "A house that faces north is cool" (a participle would save a word: "A house facing north is cool"). *That* is tolerable; *which* is downright oppressive. *Which* should signal the nonrestrictive clause (the afterthought): "The house, which faces north, is a good buy." Here you need *which.* Even restrictive clauses must turn to *which* when complicated parallels arise. "He preaches the brotherhood of man *that* everyone affirms" elaborates like this: "He preaches the brotherhood of man *which* everyone affirms, *which* all the great philosophies support, but *for which* few can make any immediate concession." Nevertheless, if you need relatives, a *that* will often ease your sentences and save you from the *which*'s.

Verbs and their derivatives, especially present participles and gerunds, can also help to cure a string of *of*'s. Alfred North White-head, usually of clear mind, once produced this linked sausage: "Education is the acquisition *of* the art *of* the utilization *of* knowledge." Anything to get around the three *of*'s and the three heavy nouns would have been better: "Education instills the art of using knowledge" — "Education teaches us to use knowledge well." Find an active verb for *is the acquisition of,* and shift *the utilization of* into some verbal form: the gerund *using,* or the infinitive *to use.* Shun the *-tion*'s! Simply change your surplus *-tion*'s and *of*'s — along with your *which* phrases—into verbs, or verbals *(to use, learning)*. You will save words, and activate your sentences.

Beware "the use of."

In fact, both *use,* as a noun, and *use,* as a verb, are dangerously wordy. Since *using* is one of our most basic concepts, other words in your sentence will already contain it:

> He uses rationalization. [He rationalizes.]
> He uses the device of foreshadowing. [He foreshadows.]
> Through [the use of] logic, he persuades.
> His [use of] dialogue is effective.

The utilization of and *utilize* are only horrendous extremes of the same pestilence, to be stamped out completely.

Break the noun habit.

Passive writing adores the noun, modifying nouns with nouns in pairs, and even in denser clusters—which then become official jargon. Break up these logjams, let the language flow, make one noun of the pair an adjective:

> *Teacher militancy* **is not as marked in Pittsburgh.** [*Teachers* **are not** so *militant* **in Pittsburgh.** *7 words for 8*]

Or convert one noun to a verb:

> *Consumer demand* **is falling in the** *service area.* [**Consumers** *are demanding* **fewer services.** *5 words for 8*]

Of course, nouns have long served English as adjectives, as in "*rail*road," "*railroad* station," "*court*house," and "*noun* habit." But modern prose has aggravated the tendency beyond belief; and we get such monstrosities as *child sex education course,* and *child sex education curriculum publications deadline reminder.* Education, sociology, and psychology produce the worst noun-stringers, the hardest for you not to copy if you take these courses. But we have all caught the habit. The nouns *level* and *quality* have produced a rash of redundancies. A meeting of "high officials" has now, unfortunately, become a meeting of "high-*level* officials," and "college courses" are now "college-*level* courses." The "finest cloth" these days is always "finest *quality* cloth." Drop those two redundant nouns and you will make a good start, and will sound surprisingly original. You can drop many an excess noun:

WORDY	DIRECT
advance notice	notice
long in size	long
puzzling in nature	puzzling
of an indefinite nature	indefinite
of a peculiar kind	peculiar
in order to	to
by means of	by
in relation to	with
in connection with	with
1978-model car	1978 car
at this point in time	at this time; now

Wherever possible, find the equivalent adjective:

of great importance	important
highest significance level	highest significant level
government spending	governmental spending
reaction fixation	reactional fixation
teaching excellence	excellent teaching
encourage teaching quality	encourage good teaching

Or change the noun to its related participle:

advance placement	advanced placement
uniform police	uniformed police
poison arrow	poisoned arrow

Or make the noun possessive:

reader interest	reader's interest
veterans insurance	veterans' insurance

Or try a cautious *of:*

color lipstick	color of lipstick
significance level	level of significance

Of all our misused nouns, *type* has become peculiarly pestilential and trite. Advertisers talk of *detergent-type cleansers* instead of *detergents;* educators, of *apprentice-type situations* instead of *apprenticeships;* newspapermen, of *fascist-type organizations* instead of *fascistic organizations.* We have forgotten that making the individual stand for the type is the simplest and oldest of metaphors: "Give us this day our daily bread." A twentieth-century supplicant might have written "bread-type food."

The active sentence transmits the message by putting each word unmistakably in its place, a noun as a noun, an adjective as an adjective, with the verb — no stationary *is* — really carrying the mail. Recently, after a flood, a newspaper produced this apparently succinct and dramatic sentence: **Dead animals cause water pollution.** (The word *cause,* incidentally, indicates wasted words.) That noun *water* as an adjective throws the meaning off and takes 25 percent more words than the essential active message: **Dead animals pollute water.** As you read your way into the sentence, it seems to say *dead animals cause water* (which is true enough), and then you must readjust your thoughts to accommodate *pollution.* The simplest change is from *water pollution* (noun-noun) to *polluted water* (adjective-noun), clarifying each word's function. But the supreme solution is to make *pollute* the verb it is, and the sentence a simple active message in which no word misspeaks itself. Here are the possibilities, in a scale from most active and clearest to most passive and wordiest, which may serve to chart your troubles if you get tangled in causes and nouns:

> Dead animals pollute water.
> Dead animals cause polluted water.
> Dead animals cause water pollution.
> Dead animals are a factor in causing the pollution of water.
> Dead animals are a serious factor in causing the water pollution situation.
> Dead farm-type animals are a danger factor in causing the post-flood clearance and water pollution situation.

So the message should now be clear. Write simple active sentences, outmaneuvering all passive eddies, all shallow *is*'s, *of*'s, *which*'s, and *that*'s, all overlappings, all rocky clusters of nouns: they take you off your course, delay your delivery, and wreck many a straight and gallant thought.

EXERCISES

1 Clear up the blurred ideas, and grammar, in these sentences from students' papers and official prose, making each word say what it means, and counting your words to make sure your version has fewer.

1. Tree pruning may be done in any season of the year.
2. After reading a dozen books, the subject is still as puzzling as ever.
3. The secret teller vote used in the past was this time a recorded teller vote.

4. The courses listed herein are those which meet the college-level requirements which were stated above.

5. Records can be used in the Audio Room by individual students for their suggested listening assignments.

6. My counter was for refunds for which the customer had already paid for.

7. Entrance was gained by means of the skylight.

8. The reason we give this test is because we are anxious to know whether or not you have reflexes that are sufficiently fast to allow you to be a safe worker.

2 Find in your textbooks two or three passages suffering from the passive voice, the *of*-and-*which* disease, the *the-use-of* contagion, and the noun habit ("which shows the effect of age and intelligence level upon the use of the reflexes and the emergence of child behavior difficulties") and rewrite them in clear English.

3 Recast these sentences in the active voice, clearing out all passive constructions, saving as many words as you can, and indicating the number saved:

1. The particular topic chosen by the instructor for study in his section of English 2 must be approved by the Steering Committee. [Start with "The Steering Committee," and don't forget the economy of an apostrophe *s*. I managed 14 words for 22.]

2. Avoidance of such blunders should not be considered a virtue for which the student is to be commended, any more than he would be praised for not wiping his hands on the tablecloth or polishing his shoes with the guest towels. [Begin "We should not"; try *avoiding* for *avoidance*. I dropped *virtue* as redundant and scored 27 for 41.]

3. The first respect in which too much variation seems to exist is in the care with which writing assignments are made. ["First, care in assigning" — 8 for 21.]

4. The remaining variations that will be mentioned are concerned not with the assignment of papers but with the marking and grading of them. ["Finally, I shall mention" — 14 for 23.]

5. The difference between restrictives and nonrestrictives can also be better approached through a study of the different contours that mark the utterance of the two kinds of elements than through confusing attempts to differentiate the two by meaning. ["One can differentiate restrictives" — I managed 13 for 38. The writer is dead wrong, incidently: meaning is the true differentiator. See p. 144.]

4 Eliminate the italicized words in the following passages, together with all their accompanying wordiness, indicating the number of words saved (my figures again are merely guides; other solutions are equally good).

1. *There is* a certain tendency to defend one's own position *which* will cause the opponent's argument to be ignored. [13 for 19]

2. *It is* the other requirements *that* present obstacles, some *of which* may prove insurmountable in the teaching of certain subjects. [11 for 20]

3. In the sort of literature-centered course being discussed here, *there is* usually a general understanding *that* themes will be based on the various literary works *that* are studied, the theory being *that* both the instruction in literature and *that* in writing will be made more effective by this interrelationship. [23 for 50]

4. The person *whom* he met was an expert *who was* able to teach the fundamentals quickly. [13 for 16]

5. They will take a pride *which is* wholly justifiable in being able to command a prose style *that is* lucid and supple. [13 for 22]

5 To culminate this chapter, clear up the wordiness, especially the italicized patches, in these two official statements, one from an eminent linguist, one from an eminent publisher.

1. The work *which is* reported *in this* study *is* an investigation *of* language *within* the social context *of* the community *in which it is spoken. It is* a study *of* a linguistic structure *which is* unusually complex, but no more than the social structure *of* the city *in which it* functions. [I tried two versions, as I chased out the *which*'s; 29 for 52, and 22 for 52.]

2. Methods *which are* unique to the historian *are illustrated* throughout the volume *in order to* show how history *is written* and how historians work. The historian's approach to his subject, *which* leads to the asking of provocative questions and to a new understanding of complex events, situations, and personalities *is probed.* The manner *in which* the historian reduces masses of chaotic fact—and occasional fancy—to reliable meaning, and the way *in which* he formulates explanations and tests them *is examined and clarified* for the student. *It is its* emphasis on historical method *which* distinguishes this book from other source readings in western civilization. The problems *which are examined* concern *themselves with* subjects *which are dealt with by* most courses in western civilization. [66 for 123]

Eight
Words

Here is the word. Sesquipedalian or short, magniloquent or low, Latin or Anglo-Saxon, Celtic, Danish, French, Spanish, Indian, Hindustani, Dutch, Italian, Portuguese, Choctaw, Swahili, Chinese, Hebrew, Turkish, Greek—English contains them all, a million words at our disposal, if we are disposed to use them. Although no language is richer than English, our expository vocabularies average probably fewer than eight thousand words. We could all increase our active vocabularies; we all have a way to go to possess our inheritance.

VOCABULARY

If you can increase your hoard, you increase your chances of finding the right word when you need it. Read as widely as you can, and look words up the second or third time you meet them. I once knew a man who swore he learned three new words a day from his reading by using each at least once in conversation. I didn't ask him about *polyphiloprogenitive* or *antidisestablishmentarianism*. It depends a little on the crowd. But the idea is sound. The bigger the vocabulary, the more various the ideas one can get across with it—the more the shades and intensities of meaning.

The big vocabulary also needs the little word. The vocabularian often stands himself on a Latin cloud and forgets the Anglo-Saxon ground—the common ground between him and his audience. So do not forget the little things, the *stuff, lint, get, twig, snap, go, mud, coax.* Hundreds of small words not in immediate vogue can refresh your vocabulary. The Norse and Anglo-Saxon adjectives in *-y (muggy, scrawny, drowsy),* for instance, rarely appear in sober print. The minute the beginner tries to sound dignified, in comes a misty layer of words a few feet off the ground and nowhere near heaven, the same two dozen or so, most of them verbs. One or two will do no harm, but any accumulation is fatal—words like *depart* instead of *go:*

accompany—go with	place—put
appeared—looked *or* seemed	possess—have
arrive—come	prepare—get ready
become—get	questioned—asked
cause—make	receive—get
cease—stop	relate—tell
complete—finish	remain—stay
continue—keep on	remove—take off
delve—dig	retire—go to bed
discover—find	return—go back
indicate—say	secure—get
locate—find	transform—change
manner—way	verify—check

Through the centuries, English has added Latin derivatives alongside the Anglo-Saxon words already there, keeping the old with the new: after the Anglo-Saxon *deor* (now *deer*) came the *beast* and then the *brute,* both from Latin through French, and the *animal* straight from Rome. We have the Anglo-Saxon *cow, sheep,* and *pig* furnishing (through French) Latin *beef, mutton,* and *pork.* Although we use more Anglo-Saxon in assembling our sentences *(to, by, with, though, is),* well over half our total vocabulary comes one way or another from Latin. The things of this world tend to be Anglo-Saxon *(man, house, stone, wind, rain);* the abstract qualities, Latin and French *(value, duty, contemplation).*

Most of our big words are Latin and Greek. Your reading acquaints you with them; your dictionary will show you their prefixes and roots. Learn the common prefixes and roots (see Exercises 1 and 2 at the end of this chapter), and you can handle all kinds of foreigners at first encounter: *con-cession* (going along with), *ex-clude* (lock out), *pre-fer* (carry before), *sub-version* (turning under), *translate* (carry across), *claustro-phobia* (dread of being locked in), *hydrophobia* (dread of water), *ailuro-philia* (love of cats), *megalo-cephalic* (big-headed), *micro-meter* (little-measurer). You can even, for fun, coin a word to suit the occasion: *megalopede* (big-footed). You can remember that *intramural* means "within the (college) walls," and that "intermural sports," which is the frequent mispronunciation and misspelling, would mean something like "wall battling wall," a physical absurdity.

Besides owning a good dictionary, you should refer, with caution, to a thesaurus, a treasury of synonyms ("together-names"), in which you can find the word you couldn't think of; the danger lies in raiding this treasury too enthusiastically. Checking for meaning in a dictionary will assure that you have expanded, not distorted, your vocabulary.

ABSTRACT AND CONCRETE

Every good stylist has perceived, in one way or another, the distinction between the abstract and the concrete. Tangible things—things we can touch—are "concrete"; their qualities, along with all our emotional, intellectual, and spiritual states, are "abstract." The rule for a good style is to be as concrete as you can, to illustrate tangibly your general propositions, to use *shoes* and *ships* and *sealing wax* instead of *commercial concomitants*.

But abstraction, a "drawing out from," is the very nature of thought. Thought moves from concrete to abstract. In fact, *all* words are abstractions. *Stick* is a generalization of all sticks, the crooked and the straight, the long and the short, the peeled and the shaggy. No word fits its object like a glove, because words are not things: words represent ideas of things. They are the means by which we class eggs and tents and trees so that we can handle them as ideas —not as actual things but as *kinds* or *classes* of things.

Abstract words can attain a power of their own, as the rhetorician heightens attention to their meanings. This ability, of course, does not come easily or soon. I repeat, you need to be as concrete as you can, to illustrate tangibly, to pin your abstractions down to specifics. But once you have learned this, you can move on to the rhetoric of abstraction, which is, indeed, a kind of squeezing of abstract words for their specific juice.

Lincoln does exactly this when he concentrates on *dedication* six times within the ten sentences of his dedication at Gettysburg: "We have come to *dedicate* . . . . It is rather for us to be here *dedicated* . . . ." Similarly, Eliot refers to "faces / Distracted from distraction by distraction" *(Four Quartets)*. Abstractions can, in fact, operate beautifully as specifics: "As a knight, Richard the Lion-Hearted was a *triumph*; as a king, he was a *disaster*."

An able writer like Samuel Johnson can make a virtual poetry of abstractions, as he alliterates and balances them against each other (I have capitalized the alliterations and italicized the balances):

> **Dryden's performances were always hasty, either** *Excited* **by some** *External occasion*, **or** *Extorted* **by some** *domestic necessity*; **he Com-Posed** *without Consideration*, **and** *Published without Correction*.

Notice especially how *excited* ("called forth") and *extorted* ("twisted out"), so alike in sound and form, so alike in making Dryden write, nevertheless contrast their opposite essential meanings.

So before we disparage abstraction, we should acknowledge its rhetorical power; and we should understand that it is an essential distillation, a primary and natural and continual mental process. Without it, we could not make four of two and two. So we make abstractions of abstractions to handle bigger and bigger groups of ideas. *Egg* becomes *food*, and *food* becomes *nourishment*. We also classify all the psychic and physical qualities we can recognize: *candor, truth, anger, beauty, negligence, temperament*. But because our thoughts drift upward, we need always to look for the word that will bring them nearer earth, that will make our abstractions seem visible and tangible, that will make them graspable — mentioning a *handle*, or a *pin*, or an *egg*, alongside our abstraction, for instance. We have to pull our abstractions down within range of our reader's own busily abstracting headpiece.

But the writer's ultimate skill perhaps lies in making a single object represent its whole abstract class. I have paired each abstraction below with its concrete translation:

> *Friendliness* **is the salesman's best asset.**
> *A smile* **is the salesman's best asset.**
>
> *Administration of proper proteins* **might have saved John Keats.**
> *A good steak* **might have saved John Keats.**
>
> **To** *understand* **the world by** *observing all of its geological details* . . . .
> **To** *see* **the world in** *a grain of sand* . . . .

METAPHOR

As you have probably noticed, I have been using metaphors — the most useful way of making our abstractions concrete. The word is

Greek for "transfer" (*meta* equals *trans* equals *across; phor* equals *fer* equals *ferry*). Metaphors illustrate our general ideas at a single stroke. Many of our common words are metaphors, *grasp* for "understanding," for instance, which compares the mind to something with hands, *transferring* the physical picture of the clutching hand to the invisible mental act.

Metaphor seems to work at about four levels, each with a different clarity and force. Suppose you wrote "he swelled and displayed his finery." You have transferred to a man the qualities of a peacock to make his appearance and personality vivid. You have chosen one of the four ways to make this transfer:

I. SIMILE: He was like a peacock.
He displayed himself like a peacock.
He displayed himself as if he were a peacock.
II. PLAIN METAPHOR: He was a peacock.
III. IMPLIED METAPHOR: He swelled and displayed his finery.
He swelled and ruffled his plumage.
He swelled, ruffling his plumage.
IV. DEAD METAPHOR: He strutted.

I. SIMILE. The simile is the most obvious form the metaphor can take, and hence would seem elementary. But it has powers of its own, particularly where the writer seems to be trying urgently to express the inexpressible, comparing his subject to several different possibilities, no one wholly adequate. In *The Sound and the Fury*, Faulkner thus describes two jaybirds (my italics):

[they] whirled up on the blast *like gaudy scraps of cloth or paper* and lodged in the mulberries, . . . screaming into the wind that *ripped* their harsh cries onward and away *like scraps of paper or of cloth in turn.*

The simile has a high poetic energy. D. H. Lawrence uses it frequently, as here in *The Plumed Serpent* (my italics):

The lake was quite black, *like a great pit.* The wind suddenly blew with violence, with a strange ripping sound in the mango trees, *as if some membrane in the air were being ripped.*

II. PLAIN METAPHOR. The plain metaphor makes its comparison in one imaginative leap. It is shorthand for "as if he were a peacock"; it pretends, by exaggeration (*hyperbole*), that he *is* a peacock. We move instinctively to this kind of exaggerated comparison as we try to convey our impressions with all their emotional impact. "He was a maniac at Frisbee," we might say, or "a dynamo." The metaphor is probably our most common figure of speech: *the pigs, the swine, a plum, a gem, a phantom of delight, a shot in the arm.* It may be humorous or bitter; it may be simply and aptly visual: "The road was a ribbon of silver." Thoreau extends a metaphor through several sentences in one of his most famous passages:

> Time is but a stream I go a-fishing in. I drink at it; but while I drink I see the sandy bottom and detect how shallow it is. Its thin current slides away, but eternity remains. I would drink deeper; fish in the sky, whose bottom is pebbly with stars.

III. IMPLIED METAPHOR. The implied metaphor is even more widely useful. It operates most often among the verbs, as in *swelled, displayed,* and *ruffled,* the verbs suggesting "peacock." Most ideas can suggest analogues of physical processes or natural history. Give your television system *tentacles* reaching into every home, and you have compared TV to an octopus, with all its lethal and wiry suggestions. You can have your school spirit *fall below zero,* and you have implied that your school spirit is like temperature, registered on a thermometer in a sudden chill. In the following passage about Hawthorne's style, Malcolm Cowley develops his explicit analogy first into a direct simile *(like a footprint)* and then into a metaphor implying that phrases are people walking at different speeds:

> He dreamed in words, while walking along the seashore or under the pines, till the words fitted themselves to his stride. The result was that his eighteenth-century English developed into a natural, a *walked,* style, with a phrase for every step and a comma after every phrase like a footprint in the sand. Sometimes the phrases hurry, sometimes they loiter, sometimes they march to drums.*

IV. DEAD METAPHOR. The art of resuscitation is the metaphorist's finest skill. It comes from liking words and paying attention to what they say. Simply add onto the dead metaphor enough implied metaphors to get the circulation going again: *He strutted, swelling and ruffling his plumage. He strutted* means by itself "walked in a pompous manner." By bringing the metaphor back to life, we keep the general meaning but also restore the physical picture of a peacock puffing up and spreading his feathers. We recognize *strut* concretely and truly for the first time. We know the word, and we know the man. We have an image of him, a posture strongly suggestive of a peacock.

* *The Portable Hawthorne* (New York: The Viking Press, 1948).

Perhaps the best dead metaphors to revive are those in proverbial clichés. See what Thoreau does (in his *Journal*) with *spur of
the moment:*

> **I feel the spur of the moment thrust deep into my side. The present
> is an inexorable rider.**

Or again, when in *Walden* he speaks of wanting "to improve the
nick of time, and notch it on my stick too," and of not being *thrown
off the track* "by every nutshell and mosquito's wing that falls on the
rails." In each case, he takes the proverbial phrase literally and
physically, adding an attribute or two to bring the old metaphor
back alive.

You can go too far, of course. Your metaphors can be too thick
and vivid, and the obvious pun brings a howl of protest. Jane
Austen disliked metaphors, as Mary Lascelles notes (*Jane Austen and
Her Art,* pp. 111–112), and reserved them for her hollow characters.
I have myself sometimes advised scholars not to use them because they are so often overworked and so often tangled in physical
impossibilities, that is, become "mixed" metaphors. "The violent
population explosion has paved the way for new intellectual growth"
looks pretty good—until you realize that explosions do not pave, and
that new vegetation does not grow up through solid pavement. The
metaphor, then, is your most potent device. It makes your thought
concrete and your writing vivid. It tells in an instant how your subject looks to you. But it is dangerous. It should be quiet, almost unnoticed, with all details agreeing, and all absolutely consistent with
the natural universe.

ALLUSION

Allusions also illustrate your general idea by referring it to something else, making it take your reader as Grant took Richmond,
making you the Mickey Mantle of the essay, or the Mickey Mouse.
Allusions depend on common knowledge. Like the metaphor, they
illustrate the remote with the familiar—a familiar place, or event, or
personage. "He looked . . . like a Japanese Humphrey Bogart,"
writes William Bittner of French author Albert Camus, and we instantly see a face like the one we know so well (a glance at Camus'
picture confirms how accurate this unusual allusion is). Perhaps the
most effective allusions depend on a knowledge of literature. When
Thoreau writes that "the winter of man's discontent was thawing as
well as the earth," we get a secret pleasure from recognizing this as

an allusive borrowing from the opening lines of Shakespeare's *Richard III:* "Now is the winter of our discontent/Made glorious summer by this sun of York." Thoreau flatters us by assuming we are as well read as he. We need not catch the allusion to enjoy his point, but if we catch it, we feel a sudden fellowship of knowledge with him. We now see the full metaphorical force, Thoreau's and Shakespeare's both, heightened as it is by our remembrance of Richard Crookback's twisted discontent, an allusive illustration of all our pitiful resentments now thawing with the spring.

Allusions can also be humorous. The hero of Peter De Vries's *The Vale of Laughter,* alluding to Lot's wife looking back on Sodom (Gen. xix.26) as he contemplates adultery for a moment, decides on the path toward home and honor.

> **If you look back, you turn into a pillar of salt. If you look ahead, you turn into a pillar of society.**

DICTION

"What we need is a mixed diction," said Aristotle, and his point remains true twenty-three centuries and several languages later. The aim of style, he says, is to be clear but distinguished. For clarity, we need common, current words; but, used alone, these are commonplace, and as ephemeral as everyday talk. For distinction, we need words not heard every minute, unusual words, large words, foreign words, metaphors; but, used alone, these become bogs, vapors, or at worst, gibberish. What we need is a diction that weds the popular with the dignified, the clear current with the sedgy margins of language and thought.

Not too low, not too high; not too simple, not too hard—an easy breadth of idea and vocabulary. English is peculiarly well endowed for this Aristotelian mixture. The long abstract Latin words and the short concrete Anglo-Saxon ones give you all the range you need. For most of your ideas, you can find Latin and Anglo-Saxon partners. In fact, for many ideas, you can find a whole spectrum of synonyms from Latin through French to Anglo-Saxon, from general to specific—from *intrepidity* to *fortitude* to *valor* to *courage* to *bravery* to *pluck* to *guts.* You can choose the high word for high effect, or you can get tough with Anglo-Saxon specifics. But you do not want all Anglo-Saxon, and you must especially guard against sobriety's luring you into all Latin. Tune your diction agreeably between the two extremes.

Indeed, the two extremes generate incomparable zip when tumbled side by side, as in *incomparable zip, inconsequential snip, megalomaniacal creep,* and the like. Rhythm and surprise conspire to set up the huge adjective first, then to add the small noun, like a monumental kick. Here is a passage from Edward Dahlberg's *Can These Bones Live,* which I opened completely at random to see how the large fell with the small (my italics):

> Christ walks on a *visonary sea;* Myshkin . . . has his ecstatic premonition of infinity when he has an *epileptic fit.* We know the inward size of an artist by his *dimensional thirsts.* . . .

This mixing of large Latin and small Anglo-Saxon, as John Crowe Ransom has noted, is what gives Shakespeare much of his power:

> This my hand will rather
> The multitudinous seas incarnadine,
> Making the green one red.

The short Anglo-Saxon *seas* works sharply between the two magnificent Latin words, as do the three short Anglo-Saxons that bring the big passage to rest, contrasting the Anglo-Saxon *red* with its big Latin kin, *incarnadine.* William Faulkner, who soaked himself in Shakespeare, gets much the same power from the same mixture. He is describing a very old Negro woman in *The Sound and the Fury* (the title itself comes from Shakespeare's *Macbeth,* the source of the *multitudinous seas* passage). She has been fat, but now she is wrinkled and completely shrunken except for her stomach:

> . . . a paunch almost dropsical, as though muscle and tissue had been courage or fortitude which the days or the years had consumed until only the indomitable skeleton was left rising like a ruin or a landmark above the somnolent and impervious guts. . . .

The impact of that short, ugly Anglo-Saxon word *guts,* with its slang metaphorical pun, is almost unbearably moving. And the impact would be nothing, the effect slurring, without the grand Latin preparation.

More on wordiness: watch for redundancies, unnecessary definitions.

Wordiness, of course, is also an offense against good diction. In speaking of sentences earlier, I commended elaboration. But I also recommended deletion as so important that we have spent a whole chapter on it. A fully worded sentence, each word in place and pulling its weight, is a joy to see. But a sentence full of words is not. Suspect every *by*, every *of*, every *which*, every *is*. Any shorter version will be clearer. I once counted the words, sentence by sentence, in a thirty-page manuscript of mine rejected as "too loose." In some sentences, I cut no more than one or two words. I rephrased many, but I think I cut no entire sentence. In fact, I added a considerable paragraph; and I still had five pages fewer, and a better essay. If you cut only one word from every sentence, you will in ten pages (if you average ten words a sentence) save your reader one whole page of uselessness and obstruction and wasted time.

Sentences can be too short and dense, of course. Many thoughts need explanation and an example or two. Many need the airing of *and*'s and *of*'s. Many simply need some loosening of phrase. In fact, colloquial phrasing, which is as clear and unnoticed as a clean window, is usually longer than its formal equivalent: *something to eat* as compared to *dinner*. By all counts, *dinner* should be better. It is shorter. It is more precise. Yet *something to eat* has social delicacy (at least as I am imagining the party). "Shall we have something to eat?" is more friendly than the more economical "Shall we have dinner?" (Similarly, in conversation we will respond "It's *me*" to avoid the spoken stiffness of grammatical correctness.) We don't want to push our friends around with precise and economical suggestions. We want them at their ease, with the choices slightly vague. Consequently, when we write *what we are after* for *object* and *how it is done* for *method*, we give our all-too-chilly prose some social warmth. These colloquial phrases use more words, but they are not wordy if they pull with the rest of the sentence.

It all comes down to redundancy, the clutter of useless words and tangential ideas—"the accumulation of words that add nothing to the sense and cloud up what clarity there is," as Aristotle says. What we write should be easy to read. Too many distinctions, too many nouns, and too much Latin can be pea soup:

> **Reading is a processing skill of symbolic reasoning sustained by the interfacilitation of an intricate hierarchy of substrata factors that have been mobilized as a psychological working system and pressed into service in accordance with the purpose of the reader.**

This comes from an educator, with the wrong kind of education. He is saying:

> **Reading is a process of symbolic reasoning aided by an intricate network of ideas and motives.**

Try *not* to define your terms. If you do, you are probably either evading the toil of finding the right word, or defining the obvious:

> Let us agree to use the word signal as an abbreviation for the phrase
> "the simplest kind of sign." (This agrees fairly well with the cus-
> tomary meaning of the word "signal.")

That came from a renowned semanticist, a student of the meaning
of words. The customary meaning of a word *is* its meaning, and un-
customary meanings come only from careful punning. Don't under-
estimate your readers, as this semanticist did.

The definer of words is usually a bad writer. Our semanticist
continues, trying to get his signals straight and grinding out about
three parts sawdust to every one of meat. In the following excerpt,
I have bracketed his sawdust. Read the sentence first as it was
written; then read it again, omitting the bracketed words:

> The moral of such examples is that all intelligent criticism [of any
> instance] of language [in use] must begin with understanding [of]
> the motives [and purposes] of the speaker [in that situation].

Here, each of the bracketed phrases is already implied in the others.
Attempting to be precise, the writer has beclouded himself. Naturally the speaker would be "in that situation"; naturally a sampling
of language would be "an instance" of language "in use." *Motives*
may not be *purposes,* but the difference here is insignificant. Our
semanticist's next sentence deserves some kind of immortality. He
means "Muddy language makes trouble":

> Unfortunately, the type of case that causes trouble in practice is
> that in which the kind of use made of language is not transparently
> clear. . . .

Clearly, transparency is hard. Writing is hard. It requires constant attention to meanings, and constant pruning. It requires a
diction a cut above the commonplace, a cut above the inaccuracies
and circumlocutions of speech, yet within easy reach. Clarity is the
first aim; economy, the second; grace, the third; dignity, the fourth.
Our writing should be a little strange, a little out of the ordinary, a
little beautiful, with words and phrases not met every day but seeming as right and natural as grass. A good diction takes care and
cultivation.

It can be overcultivated. It may seem to call attention to itself
rather than to its subject. Suddenly we are aware of the writer at
work, and a little too pleased with himself, reaching for the elegant
cliché and the showy phrase. Some readers find this very fault with
my own writing, though I do really try to saddle my maverick love
of metaphor. If I strike you in this way, you can use me profitably

as a bad example along with the following passage. I have italicized elements that individually may have a certain effectiveness, but that cumulatively become mannerism, as if the writer were watching himself gesture in a mirror. Some of his phrases are redundant; some are trite. Everything is somehow cozy and grandiose, and a little too nautical.

> *There's* **little excitement** *ashore* **when merchant ships from** *far-away* **India, Nationalist China, or Egypt** *knife through* **the** *gentle swells* **of Virginia's Hampton Roads. This** *unconcern* **may simply reflect the** *nonchalance* **of people who live by** *one of the world's great seaports.* **Or perhaps** *it's just* **that** *folk* **who** *dwell* **in the** *home towns* **of atomic submarines and Mercury astronauts are not likely to be impressed by a visiting freighter,** *from however distant a realm.* . . . *Upstream a bit* **and also** *to port,* **the mouth of the Elizabeth River leads to Portsmouth and a major naval shipyard.** *To starboard lies* **Hampton, where at Langley Air Force Base the National Aeronautics and Space Administration prepares to send a man** *into the heavens.*

EXERCISES

1 Look up in your dictionary six of the Latin and Greek constituents listed below. Illustrate each with several English derivatives closely translated, as in these two examples: *con-* (*"with"*) — *convince* (conquer with), *conclude* (shut with), *concur* (run with); *chron-* (time): chronic (lasting a long time), chronicle (a record of the time), chronometer (time-measurer).

   LATIN: *a-* (*ab-*), *ad-, ante-, bene-, bi-, circum-, con-, contra-, di-* (*dis-*), *e-* (*ex-*), *in-* (*two meanings*), *inter-, intra-, mal-, multi-, ob-, per-, post-, pre-, pro-, retro-, semi-, sub-* (*sur-*), *super-, trans-, ultra-.*

   GREEK: *a-* (*an-*), *-agogue, allo-, anthropo-, anti-, apo-, arch-, auto-, batho-, bio-, cata-, cephalo-, chron-, -cracy, demo-, dia-, dyna-, dys-, ecto-, epi-, eu-, -gen, geo-, -gon, -gony, graph-, gyn-, hemi-, hepta-, hetero-, hexa-, homo-, hydr-, hyper-, hypo-, log-, mega-, -meter, micro-, mono-, morph-, -nomy, -nym, -pathy, penta-, -phagy, phil-, -phobe (ia), -phone, poly-, pseudo-, psyche-, -scope, soph-, stereo-, sym-* (*syn-*), *teletetra-, theo-, thermo-, tri-, zoo-.*

2 Think up and look up four or five words, or as many as you can (omitting mere parts of speech, like *acts, acted, acting*) to add to the list of derivations already started after each of the following Latin verbs and their past participles. Add a note to explain any particularly interesting one like *actuary* (an insurance expert), which will turn up in your first list.

agere, actus (do) — agent, act . . .
audire, auditus (hear) — audit . . .
capere, captus (seize) — capable . . .
ducere, ductus (lead) — produce . . .
ferre, latus (carry) — infer, relate . . .
gradi, gressus (step) — grade, digression . . .
mittere, missus (send) — permit, mission . . .
pendere, pensus (hang) — depend, pension . . .
vertere, versus (turn) — diverting, verse . . .
videre, visus (see) — divide, visible . . .

3 Write three sentences using abstractions concretely, for example, "As a knight, Richard was *a triumph;* as a king, he was *a disaster.*"

4 Write three sentences in which a single concrete item represents its whole abstract class, as in "A *good steak* might have saved John Keats."

5 Write two sentences illustrating each of the following (six sentences in all): (1) the simile, (2) the plain metaphor, (3) the implied metaphor.

6 Write a sentence for each of the following dead metaphors, bringing it to life by adding implied metaphorical detail, as in "She *bridled, snorting* and *tossing her mane,*" or by adding a simile, as in "He was *dead* wrong, *laid out like a corpse on a slab.*"

dead center, pinned down, sharp as a tack, stick to, whined, purred, reflected, ran for office, yawned, take a course.

7 Revise the following sentences so as to clear up the illogical or unnatural connections in their metaphors and similes.

1. The book causes a shock, like a bucket of icy water suddenly thrown on a fire.

2. The whole social fabric will become unstuck.

3. His last week had mirrored his future, like a hand writing on the wall.

4. The recent economic picture, which seemed to spell prosperity, has wilted beyond repair.

8 Write a sentence for each of the following, in which you allude either humorously or seriously to:

1. A famous — or infamous — person (Caesar, Napoleon, Barnum, Lincoln, Stalin, Picasso, Bogart)

2. A famous event (the Declaration of Independence, the Battle of Waterloo, the Battle of the Bulge, the signing of the Magna Carta, Custer's Last Stand, the eruption of Vesuvius)

3. A notable place (Athens, Rome, Paris, London Bridge, Jerusalem)

4. This famous passage from Shakespeare, by quietly borrowing some
   of its phrases:

> To be, or not to be — that is the question:
> Whether 'tis nobler in the mind to suffer
> The slings and arrows of outrageous fortune,
> Or to take arms against a sea of troubles,
> And by opposing end them.

9 Write a paragraph in which you mix your diction as effectively as you can,
with the big Latin word and the little Anglo-Saxon, the formal word and
just the right touch of slang, working in at least two combinations of the
extremes, on the pattern of *multitudinous seas, diversionary thrust, incomparable zip,* underlining these for your instructor's convenience.

10 Write a TERRIBLE ESSAY. Have some fun with this perennial favorite, in which
you reinforce your sense for clear, figurative, and meaningful words by
writing the muddiest and wordiest essay you can invent, gloriously working
out all your bad habits. Make it a parody of the worst kind of sociological and bureaucratic prose. Here are the rules:

1. Put EVERYTHING in the passive voice.

2. Modify nouns *only* with nouns, preferably in strings of three or four,
   never with adjectives: *governmental spending* becomes *government
   level spending;* an *excellent idea* becomes *quality program concept.*

3. Use only big abstract nouns — as many *-tion*'s as *possible.*

4. Use no participles: not *dripping faucets* but *faucets which drip;* and
   use as many *which*'s as possible.

5. Use as many words as possible to say the least.

6. Work in as many trite and wordy expressions as possible: *needless to
   say, all things being equal, due to the fact that, in terms of, as far as that
   is concerned.*

7. Sprinkle heavily with *-wise-*type and *type-*type expressions, and say
   hopefully every three or four sentences.

8. Compile and use a basic terrible vocabulary: *situation, aspect, function, factor, phase, process, procedure, utilize, the use of,* and so on. The
   class may well cooperate in this.

11 Refine your sense of diction and meanings still further by writing an
IRONIC ESSAY, saying the opposite of what you mean, as in "The party was a
dazzling success," "The Rockheads are the solidest group in town," "Our
team is the best in the West."

Nine
Research

Now to consolidate and advance. Instead of eight or nine hundred words, you will write three thousand. Instead of a self-propelled debate or independent literary analysis, you will write a scholarly argument. You will also learn to use the library, and to take notes and give footnotes. You will learn the ways of scholarship. You will learn to acknowledge your predecessors as you distinguish yourself, to make not only a bibliography but a contribution.

The research paper is very likely not what you think it is. *Research* is searching again. You are looking, usually, where others have looked before; but you hope to see something they have not. Research is not combining a paragraph from the *Encyclopaedia Britannica* and a paragraph from *The Book of Knowledge* with a slick pinch from *Time*. That's robbery. Nor is it research even if you carefully change each phrase and acknowledge the source. That's drudgery. Even in some high circles, I am afraid, such scavenging is called research. It is not. It is simply a cloudier condensation of what you have done in school as a "report"—sanctioned plagiarism to teach something about ants or Ankara, a tedious compiling of what is already known. That such material is new to you is not the issue: it is already in the public stock.

CHOOSING YOUR SUBJECT

Find a thesis.

Well, then, with facts in the public stock and ideas with other people's names on them, what can you do? You move from facts and old ideas to new ideas, or to new emphasis on old ideas. Here the range is infinite. Every old idea needs new assertion. Every new assertion needs judgment. Here you are in the area of values, where everyone is in favor of virtue but in doubt about what is virtuous. Your best area for research is in some controversial issue, where you can add, and document, a new judgment of "right" or "wrong." For example, "Women's Rights" can become "Women's Changing Rôles and Language," a survey of changes in vocabulary, such as "chairman" to "chairperson," the rejection of the universal pronoun "his," and so on. You can give views approving and opposing such changes, and make your own stand, which would also be your thesis.

Make your thesis first, *before you begin research.* Call it a hypothesis (a "subthesis") if that will make you comfortable. If the hypothesis proves wrong, the testing will have furnished means to make it more nearly right. (This testing, too, will tell you if you are pursuing a subject too large to be confined in a manageable paper.) With the research paper, if you do not have a thesis to lead you through the twists and turns of print, you will never come out the other end. Unless you have a working hypothesis to keep your purpose alive as you collect, or at least a clear question to be answered, you may collect forever, forever hoping for a purpose. If you have a thesis, you will learn — and then overcome — the temptations of collecting only the supporting evidence and ignoring the obverse facts and whispers of conscience. If further facts and good arguments persuade you to the other side, so much the better. You will be the stronger for it.

Persuade your reader you are right.

You do not search primarily for facts. You do not aim to summarize everything ever said on the subject. You aim to persuade your reader that the thesis you believe in is right. You persuade him by (1) letting him see that you have been thoroughly around the subject and that you know what is known of it and thought of it, (2) showing him where the wrongs are wrong, and (3) citing the rights as right. *Your* opinion, *your* thesis, is what you are showing; all your quotations from all the authorities in the world are subservient to *your* demonstration. You are the reigning authority. You have, for the moment, the longest perspective and the last word. So, pick a thesis, and move into the library.

USING THE LIBRARY

Start with encyclopedias.

Find the *Encyclopaedia Britannica,* and you are well on your way. The *Britannica* will survey your subject. Each article will refer you, at the end, to several authorities. If someone's initials appear at the end, look them up in the contributors' list. The author of the article is an authority himself; you should mention him in your paper, and look him up later to see what books he has written on the subject. Furthermore, the contributors' list will name several works, which will swell your bibliography and aid your research. The index will also refer you to data scattered through all the volumes. Under "Medicine," for instance, it directs you to such topics as "Academies," "Hypnotism," "Licensing," "Mythology," and so on. The *Encyclopedia Americana, Collier's Encyclopedia,* and *Chamber's Encyclopaedia,* though less celebrated, will here and there challenge *Britannica's* reign, and the one-volume *Columbia Encyclopedia* is a fine shorter reference.

The World Almanac and Book of Facts, a paperbacked lode of news and statistics (issued yearly since 1868) can provide a factual nugget for almost any subject. Other good ones are *Webster's Biographical Dictionary* and *Webster's New Geographical Dictionary;* their concise entries lead quickly to thousands of people and places. And don't overlook the atlases: *The Times Atlas of the World, The National Atlas of the United States.* Another treasure-trove is *The Oxford English Dictionary* (twelve volumes and supplement—abbreviated *OED* in footnotes), which gives the date a word, like *highwayman,* first appeared in print, and traces changing usages through the years.

Explore your library's reference works. You will find many encyclopedias, outlines, atlases, and dictionaries providing more intensive coverage than the general works on the arts, history, philosophy, literature, the social sciences, the natural sciences, business, and the technologies. Instructors in subjects you may be exploring can guide you to the best references.

Next find the card catalog.

The catalog's 3 × 5 cards list all the library's holdings—books, magazines, newspapers, atlases—and alphabetize (1) authors, (2) publications, and (3) general subjects, from *A* to *Z*. You will find

John Adams and *The Anatomy of Melancholy* and *Atomic Energy,* in that order, in the *a* drawers. Page 89 illustrates the three kinds of cards (filed alphabetically) on which the card catalog will list the same book—by author, by subject, and by title.

You will notice that the bottom of the card shows the Library of Congress's cataloging number (Q175.W6517) and the number from the older, but still widely used, Dewey Decimal System (501). Your library will use one or the other, to make its own "call number," typed in the upper left corner of its cards—the number you will put on your slip when you sign out the book.

Learn the catalog's inner arrangements.

Since some alphabetical entries run on, drawer after drawer— *New York City, New York State, New York Times,* for instance— knowing the arrangements *within* these entries will help you find your book.

1. Not only men and women but organizations and institutions can be "authors" if they publish books or magazines:

> **Parke, Davis & Company, Detroit**
> **The University of Michigan**
> **U.S. Department of State**

2. Initial *A, An, The,* and their foreign equivalents (*Ein, El, Der, Une,* and so forth) are ignored in alphabetizing a title: *A Long Day in a Short Life* is alphabetized under *L.* But French surnames are treated as if they were one word: *De la Mare* as if *Delamare, La Rochefoucauld* as if *Larochefoucauld.*

3. Cards are usually alphabetized *word by word: Stock Market* comes before *Stockard* and *Stockbroker.* "Short before long" is another way of putting it, meaning that *Stock* and all its combinations with separate words precede the longer words beginning with *Stock-.* Whether a compound word is one or two makes the apparent disorder. Hyphenations are treated as two words. The sequence would run thus:

> **Stock**
> **Stock-Exchange Rulings**
> **Stock Market**
> **Stockard**

4. Cards on one subject are arranged alphabetically by author. Under *Anatomy,* for instance, you will run from "Abernathy, John" to "Yutzy, Simon Menno," and then suddenly run into a title—*An*

Author Card:
the "Main Entry"

call number:

Dewey class

author's initial

author's name and dates

title

place, publisher, and date of publication

number of pages

size of book

subject heading

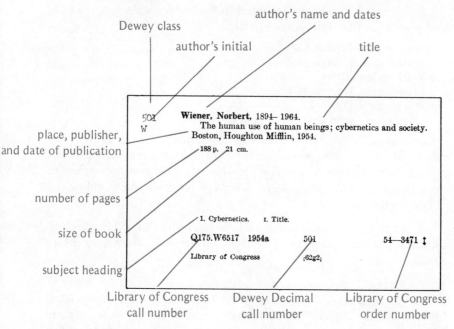

501
W

Wiener, Norbert, 1894– 1964.
   The human use of human beings; cybernetics and society.
Boston, Houghton Mifflin, 1954.

188 p.   21 cm.

1. Cybernetics.   ɪ. Title.

Q175.W6517   1954a   501   54—3471 ⵗ

Library of Congress   ₍62g2₎

Library of Congress
call number

Dewey Decimal
call number

Library of Congress
order number

Subject Card

subject heading

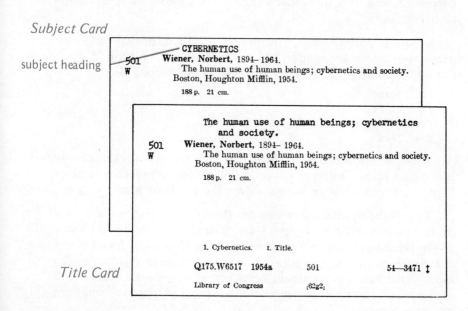

CYBERNETICS
Wiener, Norbert, 1894– 1964.
   The human use of human beings; cybernetics and society.
Boston, Houghton Mifflin, 1954.

188 p.   21 cm.

501
W

The human use of human beings; cybernetics and society.

501
W

Wiener, Norbert, 1894– 1964.
   The human use of human beings; cybernetics and society.
Boston, Houghton Mifflin, 1954.

188 p.   21 cm.

1. Cybernetics.   ɪ. Title.

Q175.W6517   1954a   501   54—3471 ⵗ

Library of Congress   ₍62g2₎

Title Card

Anatomy of Conformity—which happens to be the next large alphabetical item after the subject *Anatomy*.

5. Identical names are arranged in the order (a) person, (b) titles and places, as they fall alphabetically.

Washington, Booker T.
Washington, George
Washington (State)
Washington, University of
Washington, D.C.
Washington Square **[by Henry James]**

"Washington," the state, precedes the other "Washingtons" because "State" (which appears on the card only in parentheses) is not treated as part of its name. The University of Washington precedes "Washington, D.C." because no words or letters actually follow the "Washington" of its title.

6. Since *Mc, M', and Mac* are all filed as if they were *Mac,* they go by the letter following them: *M'Coy, McDermott, Machinery, Mac-Kenzie.*

7. Other abbreviations are also filed as if spelled out: *Dr. Zhivago* would be filed as if beginning with *Doctor; St.* as if *Saint; Mrs. Miniver* as if *Mistress*—except that many libraries now alphabetize *Mr.* and *Mrs.* as spelled, and *Ms.* has found its place in the alphabetizing.

8. Saints, popes, kings, and people are filed, in that order, by name and not be appellation (do not look under *Saint* for St. Paul, nor under *King* for King Henry VIII). The order would be:

Paul, Saint
Paul VI, Pope
Paul I, Emperor of Russia
Paul, Jean

9. An author's books are filed first by collected works, then by individual titles. Different editions of the same title follow chronologically. Books *about* an author follow the books *by* him.

That is the system. Now you can thumb through the cards filed under your subject—"Cancer," or "Television," or "Melville"—to see what books your library has on it, and you can look up any authorities your encyclopedia has mentioned. Two or three of the most recent books will probably give you all you want, because each of these will refer you, by footnote and bibliography, to important previous works.

Find the indexes to periodicals and newspapers.

Indexes to periodicals do for articles what the card catalog does for books. Some index by subjects only, others by subjects and authors. Begin with the *Reader's Guide to Periodical Literature* — an index of articles (and portraits and poems) in more than one hundred magazines. Again, take the most recent issue, look up your subject, and make yourself a bibliographical card for each title — spelling out the abbreviations of titles and dates according to the key just inside the cover. If you don't spell them out fully, your cards may be mysteries to you when you sit down to write. You can drop back a few issues and years to collect more articles; and if your subject belongs to the recent past (after 1907), you can drop back to the right year and track your subject forward. (*Poole's Index to Periodical Literature* provides similar guidance to American and English periodicals from 1802 to 1906.)

You can do the same with the *New York Times Index,* beginning with 1913. It will probably lead you to news that appeared in any paper. The *Social Sciences Index* and the *Humanities Index* do for scholarly journals what the *Reader's Guide* does for the popular ones. (These two *Indexes* were the *International Index* [until 1965] and the *Social Sciences and Humanities Index* [until 1974].) If you are searching for an essay that may be in a book rather than a magazine, your guide is the *Essay and General Literature Index.* Add to these the *Book Review Digest* (since 1905), the *Biography Index* (which nicely collects scattered references), and the *Current Biography Index,* and you will probably need no more. But if you should need more, consult Constance M. Winchell's *Guide to Reference Books,* which is also a valuable guide to encyclopedias and dictionaries.

MAKING YOUR CARDS

Before you start toward the library, get some 3 × 5 cards for your bibliography. Plan on some ten or fifteen sources for your three thousand words of text. As you pick up an author or two, and some titles, start a bibliographical card for each: *one card for each title.* Leave space to the left to put in the call number later, and space at the top for a label of your own, if needed. Put the author (last name first) on one line, and the title of his work on the next, leaving space to fill in the details of publication when you get to the work itself — for books, place of publication, publisher, and date; for magazine articles, volume number, date, and pages. Italicize (that is, underscore) titles of books and magazines; put titles of articles *within* books and magazines in quotation marks. The card catalog will supply the call numbers, and much of the other publishing data you need; but check and complete all your publishing data when you finally get the book or magazine in your hands, putting a light ✔ in pencil to assure yourself that your card is authoritative, that quotations are word for word and all your publishing data accurate, safe to check your finished paper against. Get the author's name as it appears on the title page, adding details in brackets, if helpful: Smith, D[elmar] P[rince]. Get all the information, to save repeated trips to the library. The completed cards and bibliography with our sample paper (pp. 106, 108, 120) will show you what you need.

Take brief notes.

Some people abhor putting notes on bibliographical cards. But the economy is well worth the slight clutter. Limiting yourself to what you can put on the front and back of one bibliographical card will restrain your notes to the sharp and manageable. You can always add another note card if you must. If you find one source offering a number of irresistible quotations, put each one separately on a 3×5 card (with author's name on each), so you can rearrange them later for writing.

However you do it, keep your notes brief. Read quickly, with an eye for the general idea and the telling point. Holding a clear thesis in mind will guide and limit your note taking. Some of your sources will need no more than the briefest summary: "Violently opposed, recommends complete abolition." This violent and undistinguished author will appear in your paper only among several others in a single footnote to one of your sentences: "Opposition, of course, has been tenacious and emphatic.[2]"

Suppose you are writing a paper to show that great books are usually not recognized at first (as the student in our sample did, pp. 105–120). You find in Randall Stewart's biography of Hawthorne that *The Scarlet Letter* was very well received. Here is a perfect piece of opposition, a *con*, to set your thesis against, to explain and qualify. But don't copy too much. Summarize the author's point, jot down some facts you might use, and copy down directly, within distinct quotation marks, only the most quotable phrase: "The leading critics were lavish in their praise" (see the first note card in our sample, p. 106).

Take care with page numbers. When your passage runs from one page to the next—from 29 over onto 30, for instance—put "(29–30)" after it, *but also mark the exact point where the page changed.* You might want to use only part of the passage and then be uncertain as to which of the pages contained it. An inverted L-bracket and the number "30" after the last word of page 29, will do nicely: "All had $\overline{30}$ occurred earlier." Do the same even when the page changes in mid-word with a hyphen: "having con- $\overline{21}$ vinced no one."

When preparing a research paper on a piece of literature, you would also make a bibliographical card for the edition you are using, and would probably need a number of note cards for summaries and quotations from the work itself—one card for each item, for convenience in sorting.

Take care against plagiarism.

If you borrow an idea, footnote your source. If you have an idea of your own and then discover that someone has beaten you to it, swallow your disappointment and footnote your predecessor. Or you can get back some of your own by saying, in a footnote, "I discover that James Smith agrees with me on this point," explaining, if possible, what Smith has overlooked, or his differing emphasis, and again giving a full citation of Smith's article for all future reference. A danger lies in copying out phrases from your source as you summarize what it says, and then incorporating them in your essay, without remembering that those phrases are not yours. The solution is, again, to take down and mark quotations accurately in your notes, or to summarize succinctly in your own words, as far away from the original as possible.

YOUR FIRST DRAFT

Plot your course.

Formal outlines, especially those made too early in the game, can take more time than they are worth, but a long paper with notes demands some planning. First, draft a beginning paragraph, incorporating your thesis. Then read through your notes, arranging them roughly in the order you think you will use them, getting the opposition off the street first. If your thesis is strongly argumentative, you can sort into three piles: *pro's, con's,* and *in-between's* (often simple facts). Now, by way of outline, you can simply make three or four general headings on a sheet of paper, with ample space between, in which you can jot down your sources in the order, *pro* and *con,* that is best for your argument. Our paper on the American classics would block out something like this:

I. Generally poor reception

PRO	CON
	Hawthorne's instant fame
But gloom, indecency	Henry James
Declining sales	
Uncle Tom	
Ben Hur	

II. Melville's poor
    sales
   Hostile English
    reviews

	London Herald
	Lewes
	The first six days in
	America
But hostility, then	
silence	

III.

	Praise for Thoreau
But not unanimous	
(Canby)	
Poor sales—Lamp-	
lighter	
Canby—nature read-	
ing	
	George Eliot
	Recognition abroad

IV. Whitman unknown

	Emerson
	Thoreau
	Lincoln
	Notoriety

Outline more fully, if you wish.

You can easily refine this rough blocking (probably more nearly complete here than yours would actually be) into a full topic outline, one that displays your points logically, not necessarily in the actual sequence of your writing. The principle of outlining is to rank equivalent headings—keeping your headings all as nouns, or noun phrases, to make the ranks apparent. You simply mark heads and subheads by alternating numbers and letters as you proceed downhill, from roman numeral *I* through capital *A* to arabic *1* and lowercase *a*, until you reach, if you need them, parenthesized *(1)* and *(a)*, and even lowercase roman numerals, *i, ii, iii,* as your very smallest subdivisions. You indent equal heads equally, aligning equivalents under equivalents, roman under roman, capital under capital, and so on. Every *A* should have its *B,* at least; and every *1* its *2.* If you have just a single heading, drop it, or absorb it into the larger heading above it.

But, *begin to write soon.* You have already begun to write, of course, in getting your thesis down on paper, and then drafting a first paragraph to hold it. Now that you have blocked out your argument, however roughly, plunge into your first draft.

Put in your references as you go.

Your first draft should have all your footnotes, abbreviated, right in the text. Otherwise you will lose your place, and go mad with numbers. Put the notes at the *end* of the last pertinent sentence. Make your quotations in full, all distinctly set within quotation marks, and include the author's surname and the page number with each citation. You will change these in your final draft, of course, filling in the names or leaving them out of the note altogether if they appear in the text. But it will help you in checking against your cards to have an author's name and a page number for each citation. *Don't number your footnotes yet.* When your draft is finished, add the numbers in pencil, so you can change them; circle them in red pencil, so you can see them. As you type along, mark your footnotes with triple parentheses: (((. . .)))—the easiest distinction you can make. See pp. 110–111 for a sample first-draft page, with its accompanying transformation into smooth and final copy.

YOUR FINAL DRAFT

Reset your long quotations.

Your final draft will change in many ways, as the rewriting polishes up your phrases and turns up new and better ideas. But some changes are merely in presentation. The triple parentheses of your first draft will disappear, along with the quotation marks around the *long* quotations, since you will single-space and indent, *without quotation marks,* all quotations of more than fifty words, to simulate the appearance of a printed page. You will do the same with shorter quotations, if you want to give them special emphasis, and also with passages of poetry. If your quotation begins as a paragraph, indent its first line farther, to reproduce the paragraphing. Again, pp. 110–111 show how a first-draft quotation is transformed in the final draft. Check the rules about quotation marks on pp. 96 and 150–151.

Allow space for notes at the foot of the page.

Some instructors like footnotes gathered all together in a section at the end, as they would be in a manuscript prepared for the printer. But many prefer them at the foot, where the reader can see them, as if on a printed page. From your preliminary draft, you can see about how many footnotes will fall on your page, and about how much space to allow at the bottom. Allow plenty. You will begin your notes three spaces below your text (you have been double-spacing your text). Do *not* type a solid line between text and notes: this indicates a footnote continued from the preceding page. Single-space each note, but double-space between notes. Indent as for a paragraph. To type the number, use the variable line-spacer and roll down about half the height of a capital letter. After typing the number, return to your normal typing line:

⁴ Stewart, p. 97.

After the first line, notes return to the left margin, as in paragraphs.

Footnotes carry only information not mentioned in the text. At first mention in text or note, give your author's full name, in normal order—"Randall Stewart"—and use only his last name thereafter. (Your alphabetized bibliography will give last name first.) If your text names the author, the note carries only the title of his work, the publishing data, and the page number. If your text names the author and his work, the note carries only the publishing data and the page number. Once you have cited a source, you can put the page numbers of further citations directly in your text, within parentheses. Note where the quotation marks go and how the period and comma follow the parenthesis:

> Henry James describes how the book "was a great success, and [Hawthorne] immediately found himself famous" (p. 108).
>
> Henry James (p. 108) describes the book's success.

At the end of a long indented, single-spaced quotation from a work already cited, the page number in parentheses *follows* the period (see the inset quotations in our sample paper):

> . . . had a mysterious charm. (p. 108)

Make and punctuate your footnotes meticulously.

The three principal kinds of references produce three forms of footnotes:

BOOK

[1]Watson G. Branch, Melville, The Critical Heritage
(London and Boston: Routledge & Kegan Paul, 1974), p. 2.

QUARTERLY MAGAZINE

[2] Ernest W. Baughman, "Public Confession and
The Scarlett Letter," The New England Quarterly,
40 (1967), 548-549.

When giving the volume number, "40," you omit the "p." or "pp." before page numbers, which I prefer in full. If you choose to abbreviate them, do it thus: "548–49," not "548–9"; "27–29," not "27–9"; but "107–8," not "107–08." Convert all Roman volume numbers into Arabic: "XL" becomes "40."

POPULAR MAGAZINE OR NEWSPAPER

[3] Norman R. Collins, "More Frenzied Fiction,"
News Chronicle, April 20, 1931, p. 4.

Ignore volume number, if any. As in this last example, give the full date for a popular magazine, instead of volume number and year, and *use no parentheses*. Newspaper articles sometimes need more detail:

[4] "The Trouble with Fiction" (editorial),
New York Times, April 10, 1984, Sec. 4, p. 8.

Notice the comma here: omitted after "Fiction" and inserted after the parenthesis. Do the same with any parenthetical explanation of a title. With this newspaper, you need to give the section number because each section begins numbering anew.

Here are some further complications:

[5] Abraham B. Caldwell, "The Case for a Streaming
Consciousness," American Questioner, June 20, 1979,
p. 37, quoted in Albert N. Mendenhall, Modern Commentary (Princeton: Little House, 1979), p. 308.

You have found the quotation in Mendenhall's book.

[6] D. C. Hill, "Who Is Communicating What?" in
Essays for Study, ed. James L. McDonald and Leonard
P. Doan (New York: Appleton Hall, 1973), p. 214;
reprinted from Era, 12 (1972).

McDonald and Doan have edited the collection, or casebook. A title
ending in a question mark should not take a comma.

[7] David R. Small, "The Telephone and Urbaniza-
tion," in Annals of American Communication, ed.
Walter Beinholt (Boston: Large, Green and Co., 1969),
III, 401.

The *Annals of American Communication* is a series of bound books,
not a magazine: the volume number is in Roman numerals, and it
follows the parenthesis. Had this been a magazine, the entry would
have omitted the "in," the editor, and the place of publication, and
would have read ". . . *Annals of American Communication,* 3 (1969),
401."

[8] Arnold Peters, "Medicine," Encyc. Brit.,
11th ed.

Abbreviate familiar titles, so long as they remain clear. You need
neither volume nor page numbers in alphabetized encyclopedias;
and only the number (*or* the year of publication) of the edition you
are citing, without parentheses. Here the article was initialed "A. P.,"
and you have looked up the author's name in the contributors' list.

[9] "Prunes," Encyc. Brit., 11th Ed.

Here the article was not initialed.

[10] George L. Gillies, "Robert Herrick's
'Corinna,'" Speculation, 2 (1881), 490.

This shows where to put the comma when the title of a magazine
article ends in a quotation, and you have to use both single and
double quotation marks. Gillies's original title would have looked
like this: Robert Herrick's "Corinna."

[11] Romeo and Juliet II.iii.94, in An Essential
Shakespeare, ed. Russell Fraser (New York: Prentice-
Hall, 1972).

Note the absence of the comma after the play's title, and the periods
and close spacing between Act.scene.line. Subsequent references

would go directly in your text within parentheses: "(IV.iii.11–12)."
Or, if you are quoting several of Shakespeare's plays: "(*Romeo*
IV.iii.11–12)." See further instructions below (p. 101).

> [12] P[aul] F[riedrich] Schwartz, A Quartet of
> Thoughts (New York: Appleton Hall, 1943), p. 7.

> [13] [George H. Lewes], "Percy Bysshe Shelley,"
> Westminster Review, 35 (April 1841), 303-344.

These two footnotes show how to use brackets to add details not
actually appearing in the published work. Of course, famous initials
are kept as initials, as with T. S. Eliot, H. G. Wells, or D. H. Lawrence.
You also need brackets to replace parentheses when your comments
in a footnote require a parenthesis around your entire source:

> [14] . . . (cited in John E. Basset, William Faulkner:
> An Annotated Checklist of Criticism [New York: David
> Lewis, 1972], p. 35).

Pamphlets and other oddities just require common sense:

> [15] "The Reading Problem," mimeographed pamphlet,
> Concerned Parents Committee, Center City, Arkansas,
> Dec. 25, 1975, p. 8.

> [16] U. S. Congress, House Committee on Health,
> Education, and Welfare, Racial Integration, 101st
> Cong., 2nd sess., 1969, H. Rep. 391 to accompany
> H. R. 6128.

Pamphlets like these you must play by instinct, including all the
details, as briefly as possible, that would help someone else hunt
them down. These examples, together with the footnotes in our
sample research paper, should cover most footnoting problems, or
suggest how you can meet them.

Abbreviate your references after the first full citation.
Two old favorite abbreviations are now mercifully out of style.
DO NOT USE:

ibid. —*ibidem* ("in the same place"), meaning the title cited in the
note directly before. Instead, USE THE AUTHOR'S LAST NAME, AND GIVE
THE PAGE.

op. cit. —*opere citato* ("in the work cited"), meaning a title referred to again after other notes have intervened. Again, USE THE
AUTHOR'S LAST NAME INSTEAD, AND GIVE THE PAGE: "Stewart, p. 97."

If you have two Stewarts, simply include their initials. If Stewart has two articles or books on Hawthorne, devise two convenient short titles for subsequent references:

^{2}Stewart, <u>Hawthorne</u>, p. 97.

^{3}Stewart, "Symbols," p. 301.

Three are still used and especially useful (do *not* italicize them):

cf.—*confer* ("bring together," or "compare"); do not use for "see."

et al.—*et alii* ("and others"); does not mean "and all"; use after the first author in multiple authorships: "Ronald Elkins et al."

loc. cit.—*loco citato* ("in the place cited"); use without page number, when you cite a page previously noted. Best in parentheses *in the text.* See p. 109.

Two more Latin terms, also not italicized, are equally handy:

passim—(not an abbreviation, but a Latin word meaning "throughout the work; here and there") use when a writer makes the same point in many places within a single work; use also for statistics you have compiled from observations and tables scattered throughout his work.

sic—a Latin word meaning "so"; "this is so"; always in brackets —[sic]—because used only within quotations following some misspelling or other surprising detail to show that it really was there, was "so" in the original, and that the mistake is not yours.

Other useful abbreviations for footnotes are:

c. or ca.	*circa,* "about" (c. 1709)
ch., chs.	chapter, chapters
ed.	edited by, edition, editor
f., ff.	and the following page, pages
l., ll.	line, lines
MS., MSS.	manuscript, manuscripts
N.B.	*nota bene* ("note well")
n.d.	no date given
n.p.	no place of publication given
p., pp.	page, pages
rev.	revised
tr., trans.	translated by
vol., vols.	volume, volumes

A footnote using some of these might go like this (you have already fully cited Weiss and Dillon):

<blockquote>
16 See Donald Allenberg et al., <u>Population</u> <u>in</u>
<u>Early</u> <u>New</u> <u>England</u> (Boston: Large, Green and Co.,
1974), pp. 308ff.; cf. Weiss, p. 60. Dillon,
passim, takes a position even more conservative than
Weiss's. See also A. H. Hawkins, ed., <u>Statistical</u>
<u>Surveys</u> (Chicago: Nonesuch Press, 1960; rev. 1973),
pp. 71-83 and ch. 10. Records sufficient for broad
comparisons begin only ca. 1850.
</blockquote>

Abbreviate books of the Bible, even the first time.

The Bible and its books, though capitalized as ordinary titles, are never italicized. Biblical references go directly into your text, within parentheses—no footnote, no commas, *lowercase* roman numerals for chapter, arabic for verse: "Mark xvi.6"; "Jer. vi.24"; "II Sam. xviii.33." No comma—only a space—separates name from numbers; periods separate the numbers, *with no spacing*. The dictionary gives the accepted abbreviations: Gen., Exod., Lev., Deut. Make biblical references like this:

<blockquote>
There is still nothing new under the sun (Eccl. i.9); man

still does not live by bread alone (Matt. iv.4).

As Ecclesiastes tells us, "there is no new thing

under the sun" (i.9).
</blockquote>

Abbreviate plays and long poems after the first time.

Handle plays and long poems like biblical citations, after an initial footnote that identifies the edition (see p. 98). Italicize the title (underscore the title with your typewriter): *"Merch.* II iv.72–75" (this is *The Merchant of Venice,* Act II, Scene iv, lines 72–75); *"Caesar* V.iii.6," *"Ham.* I.i.23," *"Iliad* IX.93, "*P.L.* IV.918" (*Paradise Lost,* Book IV, line 918). Use the numbers alone if you have already mentioned the title, or have clearly implied it, as in repeated quotations from the same work.

Match your bibliography to your footnotes.

When your paper is finally typed, arrange the cards of the works cited in your footnotes in alphabetical order (by authors' last names or, with anonymous works, by first words of titles—ignoring initial *The, A,* or *An*). You will not have used all your notes, nor all the articles you have carded. In typing your bibliography, pass over them in decent silence. *Include no work not specifically cited.* Your bibliographical entries will be just like your footnotes except that: (1) you will put the author's last name first; (2) you will give the total span of pages for magazine articles—none at all for books; (3) you will reverse indentation so that the author's name will stand out; and (4) you will punctuate differently—putting one period after the alphabetized name or title, and another (no parentheses) after a book's place and date of publication. Here are some special cases:

```
Hill, D. C.  "Who Is Communicating What?" in Essays
     for Study, ed. James L. McDonald and Leonard P.
     Doan.  New York: Appleton Hall, 1973.  Pp. 211-
     219.  Reprinted from Era, 12 1972), 9-18.
```

Notice the capitalized "Pp. 211–219." Since this article is in a book, the publishing data have required a period after "1973." When listing other works by the same author, use a solid line (your underscorer) and a period:

```
Jones, Bingham.  The Kinescopic Arts and Sciences.
     Princeton: Little House, 1970.

     ————.  "Television and Vision: The Case for Govern-
     mental Control," Independent Review, 7 (1969),
     18-31.
```

Alphabetize by the name of the *author,* not the editor of collections:

```
Small, David R.  "The Telephone and Urbanization,"
     in Annals of American Communication, ed. Walter
     Beinholt.  Boston: Large, Green and Co., 1969.
     III, 398-407.
```

But alphabetize by the name of the editor, when you have referred to his Introduction and notes:

```
Cowley, Malcolm.  The Portable Hawthorne, ed., with
     Introduction and Notes.  New York: Viking Press,
     1948.
```

Alphabetize by the first significant word in anonymous works ("Trouble" in the following example):

```
"The Trouble with Puritans," Anon. editorial, The
     New York Times, April 10, 1984, Sec. 4, p. 8.
```

I have based these instructions on the current edition of *The MLA Style Sheet* (compiled by the Modern Language Association of America), following the customs for work in literature and the humanities. The sciences use slightly different conventions. An article would look like this in a botanical bibliography (no quotation marks, no parentheses, fewer capitals):

```
Mann, K. H.  1973.  Seaweeds: their productivity
     and strategy for growth.  Science 182: 975-981.
```

A good general manual is Kate L. Turabian, *A Manual for Writers of Term Papers, Theses, and Dissertations,* Fourth Edition (Chicago and London: The University of Chicago Press, 1973). For some advanced courses, you may also want to consult:

Conference of Biological Editors. *CBE Style Manual.* Washington, D.C.: American Institute of Biological Sciences, 1972.

CRC Handbook of Chemistry and Physics. 56th ed. Ed. Robert C. Weast. Cleveland: Chemical Rubber Co., 1975.

A Manual of Style. 12th ed, rev. Chicago and London: The University of Chicago Press, 1969.

Publication Manual of the American Psychological Association. Washington, D.C.: American Psychological Association, Inc., 1974.

Style Manual. Rev. ed. Washington, D.C.: U.S. Government Printing Office, 1973.

SAMPLE RESEARCH PAPER

Here is a sample, a complete research paper from one of my classes, to show what the final product can look like. I had suggested, among several topics, that the unusual cluster of four of America's greatest books in the 1850's might be worth looking into. A few students took one or another of the books, defined its quality as they and several modern critics saw it, and then checked that against the early reactions. This student took all four books, going first to the *Encyclo-*

paedia Britannica, then to the leading biographies. I had also suggested that the 1911 *Britannica* was particularly strong on literary topics falling before that date. From a reference to *Uncle Tom's Cabin* in one of the books, without sales figures, the student simply went to the S shelf and found in Mrs. Stowe's introduction to a later edition the figures he wanted.

To convey an idea of the whole process, the backs of the first two pages show bibliographical cards with notes, corresponding to the first four footnotes, and the back of the third page (opposite p. 3 of the paper) shows a page of the first draft, which matches the final text beginning with the James quotation at the bottom of p. 2.

This research paper, for the most part, follows the conventional format: title page with outline (unnumbered if one page, numbered with Roman numerals if more than one page); double-spaced text with single-spaced footnotes, each page except the first numbered in Arabic at the top; and the bibliography at the end, on a separate page or pages. Our paper combines title page with outline; perhaps more common is a separate title page. To set up a separate title page, center the title on the width of the page somewhat above the middle and the other elements—name, designation of course, instructor's name, date—below as shown:

AMERICA'S CLASSICS:

WHEN 1850 WAS TODAY

Vincent Cross

[12 to 15 lines of space]

English 270

Mr. Baker

April 16, 1976

Our bibliography is alphabetized by authors' last names or by titles when the author is unknown or anonymous. Keeping this alphabetization for each group, you can divide a longer bibliography into *primary sources*—works of literature, historical documents, letters, and so on— and *secondary sources,* or works *about* your subject.

Vincent Cross
English 270
Mr. Baker
April 16, 1976

AMERICA'S CLASSICS: WHEN 1850 WAS TODAY

Thesis: Though some readers recognized their greatness, all

four of America's classics of the 1850's went into

a fairly early eclipse.

I. Hawthorne's <u>The Scarlet Letter</u> (1850)   *Topic*
    A. Instant fame   *Outline*
        1. Fields's enthusiasm
        2. Early reviews
            a. Favorable
            b. Unfavorable
        3. Henry James's recollection
    B. Low sales as against best sellers

II. Melville's <u>Moby-Dick</u> (1851)
     A. Mixed but balanced reception
         1. England
             a. Favorable
             b. Unfavorable
         2. America's early praise turned sour
     B. The almost total eclipse

III. Thoreau's <u>Walden</u> (1854)
      A. Mixed reception
      B. America's neglect
      C. George Eliot and growing recognition abroad

IV. Whitman's <u>Leaves of Grass</u> (1855)
     A. Total silence
     B. Whitman's gift-copies and self-advertising
     C. Influential readers
         1. Emerson
         2. Thoreau
         3. Lincoln
     D. Notoriety and fame

828   Stewart, Randall
H40   <u>Nathaniel Hawthorne</u> : <u>A</u>
S85   <u>Biography</u> (New Haven : Yale
1961   University Press, 1948)

1st ed., March 16, 1850-2,000 copies sold
in 10 days.
2nd ed., 3,000 copies, sales good at first, soon
dropped. 2 yrs. later <u>SL</u> advertised
as in its "sixth thousandth" (96).
"The leading critics were lavish in their
praise." ✓(97)

828   James, Henry
H40   <u>Hawthorne</u> (Ithaca : Cornell Univ.
J27   Press, 1967 -- first printed 1879)
1967

James qts. James .T. Fields (H's publisher). F. called
on H. in Salem, found him depressed. H. gives him
unfinished MS. of <u>Scarlet Letter</u> ("thrust
upon him") as he was leaving. H.
depressed because earlier stories not
well nor widely received. F. goes back
to Boston, reads MS. with mounting

excitement. Sends letter saying so and
announcing his return next day to
arrange publication. When he arrived:
   "I went on in such an amazing
state of excitement... that he would
not believe I was really in earnest.
He seemed to think I was beside
myself, & laughed sadly at my
enthusiasm." ✓ (107)

AMERICAN CLASSICS: WHEN 1850 WAS TODAY

In the eighteen-fifties, American literature came of *Beginning*
age. Four of America's greatest books appeared in the first
five years of that decade: Nathaniel Hawthorne's The Scarlet Letter (1850), Herman Melville's Moby-Dick (1851), Henry
David Thoreau's Walden (1854), and Walt Whitman's Leaves of
Grass (1855). But was their greatness recognized at the *(Funneling to)*
time? Would we recognize them today? How did these new and
unknown books seem to the reviewers who received them or
the people who bought them? Were they best sellers? Actually, none of them was. Though each of them had readers
who recognized their quality, all of them also received
negative criticism, some very severe, and all went into a
fairly early eclipse.

Hawthorne's The Scarlet Letter (1850) is the nearest *Opposition*
to an exception to this rule. Randall Stewart reports that
the leading critics were lavish in their praise,[1] reflecting
the same enthusiasm that James T. Fields, Hawthorne's publisher, had felt on reading the unfinished manuscript.
Fields tells of calling on Hawthorne in Salem, finding him
depressed, having the unfinished manuscript given him on
leaving, and reading it that night with growing excitement.
He returned to Salem the next day to arrange for publication: "I went on in such an amazing state of excitement

[1]Nathaniel Hawthorne: A Biography (New Haven: Yale *Footnote: Author Named in Text*
University Press, 1948), p. 97.

ALL ON
ONE SIDE

828   Hawthorne, Julian
H 40   _Hawthorne and His Circle_ (New
H39h   York : Harper & Bros., 1903)

"One day a big man, with a broken beard
and shining brown eyes, who bubbled
over with enthusiasm and fun, made his
appearance and talked voluably about something &
went away again, & my father & mother smiled at each
other. _The SL_ had been written, and James T. Fields
had read it, & declared it the greatest bk. of the age."✓(18)

SECOND
"STEWART"
CARD —
FRONT

Stewart—   ②
E. P. Whipple (_Graham's Mag._) answered objections of
gloominess : "The Custom House" showed H's ability
to mix tragedy & comedy, like Shakespeare, but hopes
"pathos and power" will be "more relieved by touches
of that beautiful and peculiar humor, so
serene and searching, in which he excells
almost all living writers." ✓ — in next bk. (97)

"A group of hostile critics were
violently proclaiming ... the gross im—

BACK

morality of the book." ✓ (97) _Brownson's_
Review, by Orestes A. Brownson, led the attack:

"There is an unsound state of public morals
when the novelist is permitted, w'out a
scorching rebuke, to select such crimes, &
to invest them w. all the fascination of
genius, and all the charms of a highly
polished style." ✓ (97)

. . . that [Hawthorne] would not believe I was really in earnest. He seemed to think I was beside myself, and laughed at my enthusiasm."[2] Julian Hawthorne, Hawthorne's son, remembers the occasion:

Ellipsis and Bracket

> One day a big man, with a brown beard and shining brown eyes, who bubbled over with enthusiasm and fun, made his appearance and talked volubly about something, and went away again, and my father and mother smiled at each other. The Scarlet Letter had been written, and James T. Fields had read it, and declared it the greatest book of the age.[3]

Extended Quotation, with Footnote

Nevertheless, even the most favorable critics thought the book was too uninterruptedly gloomy. E. P. Whipple, who compared Hawthorne to Shakespeare for mixing the comic tone of "The Custom House" section with the tragic main story, hoped that in Hawthorne's next book the "pathos and power" would be "more relieved by touches of that beautiful and peculiar humor, so serene and searching, in which he excels almost all living writers."[4] Moreover, hostile critics attacked the book as immoral, especially Orestes A. Brownson in Brownson's Review:

Topic Sentence

> There is an unsound state of public morals when the novelist is permitted, without a scorching rebuke, to select such crimes, and to invest them with all the fascination of genius, and all the charms of a highly polished style. (loc. cit.)

Extended Quotation; Loc. Cit. Reference to Stewart

Henry James best describes how the book "was a great

[2]Henry James, Hawthorne (Ithaca: Cornell University Press, 1967, first published 1879), p. 107.

Author Not Named in Text

[3]Hawthorne and His Circle (New York: Harper & Brothers, 1903), p. 18.

[4]Stewart, p. 97.

Second Citation Abbreviated

and to the forefront of it" (p. 109). Henry James ~~reports~~ *writes* that:

> The writer of these lines, who was a child at the time,
> remembers dimly the sensation the book produced, and the
> little shudder with which people alluded to it, as if a
> peculiar horror were mixed with its attractions. He was
> too young to read it himself, but its title, upon which
> he fixed his eyes as the book lay upon the table, had
> a mysterious charm. (p. 108)

Little Henry thought of the "scarlet letter" as a red envelope being sent

~~James wondered why a letter should be crimson~~, until later his *through the mails*

mother showed him a painting in the National Gallery of Hester

teasingly

and her scarlet A, with little Pearl touching it, which indicates

already

the fame the book had achieved.

But the great acclaim died down. Sales soon dropped off.

(March 16, 1850) had

The first edition of 2,000 copies sold out in ten days, but the

second edition of 3,000 began to slow down. Two years later,

the publishers advertised that the book was in its "sixth

⑤

thousandth." (((Stewart, p. 96.))) This is almost nothing

compared to Uncle Tom's Cabin (1852), which sold 10,000 copies

to

"in a few days" and over 300,000 in the first year, or Ben Hur,

⑥

which sold 200,000 copies in 1887. (((Harriet Beecher Stowe,

"The Author's Introduction," Uncle Tom's Cabin, or, Life Among

the Lowly (Boston and New York: Houghton Mifflin and Co., 1896),

p. lxii; Hugh W. Hetherington, Melville's Reviewers, British and

American, 1846-1891 (Chapel Hill: University of North Carolina

Press, 1961), p. 221.)))

was almost

Melville's Moby-Dick sold even more poorly, and soon ~~nobody~~

completely forgotten.

~~was reading it.~~ It was published first in London as The Whale

and additions,

(October 16, 1851), and then, with ~~some~~ revisions, it was published

in America as Moby-Dick (November 14, 1851). Many readers were

in not finding

disappointed ~~to find that it did not have~~ the adventures they success, and [Hawthorne] immediately found himself famous" (p. 108). There was a general pride "in the idea of America having produced a novel that belonged to literature, and to the forefront of it" (p. 109). James writes:

> The writer of these lines, who was a child at the time, remembers dimly the sensation the book produced, and the little shudder with which people alluded to it, as if a peculiar horror were mixed with its attractions. He was too young to read it himself, but its title, upon which he fixed his eyes as the book lay upon the table, had a mysterious charm. (p. 108)

Little Henry thought of the "scarlet letter" as a red envelope being sent through the mails, until his mother showed him a painting in the National Gallery of Hester and her scarlet A, with little Pearl touching it teasingly, which indicates the fame the book had already achieved.

But the great acclaim died down. Sales soon dropped off. The first edition of 2,000 copies (March 16, 1850) had sold out in ten days, but the second edition of 3,000 began to slow down. Two years later, the publishers advertised that the book was in its "sixth thousandth."[5] This is almost nothing compared to Uncle Tom's Cabin (1852), which sold 10,000 copies "in a few days" and over 300,000 in the first year, or to Ben Hur, which sold 200,000 copies in 1887.[6]

[5]Stewart, p. 96.

[6]Harriet Beecher Stowe, "The Author's Introduction," Uncle Tom's Cabin, or, Life Among the Lowly (Boston and New York: Houghton Mifflin and Co., 1896), p. lxii; Hugh W. Hetherington, Melville's Reviewers, British and American, 1846-1891 (Chapel Hill: University of North Carolina Press, 1961), p. 221.

Supporting View; Further References in Parentheses, Followed by Period

Quotation from Work Already Cited, with Reference in Parentheses at End, Not Followed by Period

Date in Parentheses

Publication Date in Parentheses

Footnote Covering Two Sources

Melville's <u>Moby-Dick</u> sold even more poorly, and soon was almost completely forgotten. It was published first in London as <u>The Whale</u> (October 16, 1851), and then, with revisions and additions, it was published in America as <u>Moby-Dick</u> (November 14, 1851). Many readers were disappointed in not finding the adventures they had expected from Melville's earlier books, and many "decried the mixture of modes and of subjects in what they considered an extravagant though often powerful production."[7] In London, both on the same day (October 25, 1851), <u>The Spectator</u> and <u>The Athenaeum</u> published hostile reviews. <u>The Athenaeum</u> called it "an ill-compounded mixture of romance and matter-of-fact," and <u>The Spectator</u> wrote:

> This sea novel is a singular medley of naval observation, magazine article writing, satiric reflection upon the conventionalisms of civilized life, and rhapsody run mad.[8]

Nevertheless, also on October 25, a review in <u>John Bull</u> praised the book:

[sic] Pointing to Error in Punctuation— Period Instead of Question Mark

> Who would have looked for philosophy in whales, or for poetry in blubber.[sic] Yet few books which professedly deal in metaphysics, or claim the parentage of the muses, contain as much true philosophy and as much genuine poetry as the tale of the <u>Pequod's</u> whaling expedition.[9]

Moreover, London's <u>Morning Herald</u>, five days earlier (October 20, 1851) had already come out with unqualified praise:

[7]Watson G. Branch, <u>Melville: The Critical Heritage</u> (London and Boston: Routlege & Kegan Paul, 1947), p. 1.

Two Pages Not Consecutive

[8]Branch, pp. 253, 257.

[9]Branch, p. 255.·

"Melville is on the right track." Melville's new book now
shows "a concentration of the whole powers of the man."
The reviewer continues:

> Resolutely discarding all that does not bear directly
> on the matter at hand, he has succeeded in painting
> such a picture--now lurid, now ablaze with splendour
> --of sea life, in its most arduous and exciting form,
> as for vigor, originality, and interest, has never
> been surpassed.[10]

George Henry Lewes, a leading critic, says that "No European

Quotation, Ellipsis at End

pen still has the power to portray the Unseen so vividly

. . . ."[11] In the three months in which the book was re-

viewed in England, says Hetherington, the reception was

Quotation Sharpened to Key Phrases

"evenly balanced," though the ultimate reception was "com-

pletely negative" (p. 201).

In America, when Moby-Dick was published on November
15, 1851, the reception was similar. On that day, The
Courier and New York Enquirer, the biggest paper in the
city of New York, praised the book's "freshness," "vivid-
ness," and "witching interest"; Melville showed "the gusto
of true genius."[12] In spite of some protests over "pro-
faneness" and "indecency," all reviewers in the first six
days were favorable.

But the tide began to turn. Soon the book was "sad
stuff, dull and dreary, or ridiculous" (p. 218). In the
first ten days, it had sold 1,835 copies, but by February

[10]Hetherington, p. 191.

[11]Hetherington, p. 196.

[12]Hetherington, p. 204.

*Date Inserted
To Help Reader*

7 of the next year (1852), it had sold only 471 more.

Thirty-six years later, through 1887, the year of Ben Hur's

200,000 copies, it had sold only 3,797. Melville's earlier

book, Typee (1846), had sold 6,392 copies in three years

(p. 221). The 1911 Encyclopaedia Britannica gives Mel-

ville only a paragraph, mentioning Moby-Dick with Typee,

Omoo, and White Jacket as portraying "seafaring life with

vigour and originality," and ends by saying that Melville

wrote in a period "when fiction written by writers below

Irving, Poe, and Hawthorne was measured by humble artistic

standards." Moby-Dick was far from the classic it is con-

sidered today.

*New Section
with Transition*

The reception of Thoreau's Walden (August 9, 1854)

was similar to that of Moby-Dick, though without the open

hostility on the negative side. "Praise . . . was hearty

but by no means unanimous."[13] On July 29, 1854, Horace

Greeley announced the forthcoming book in the New York

Tribune, a widely read and very influential paper, with a

*Loc. Cit.
Reference
to Canby*

summary and extracts of about 2,000 words (loc. cit.), and

long approving reviews appeared in Graham's Magazine and

Putnam's Monthly.[14] But sales were poor. In the same

year that Maria Cummins's sentimental novel The Lamplighter

became a tremendous success, Walden's 2,000 copies were

---

[13]Henry Seidel Canby, Thoreau (Boston: Houghton Mifflin Co., 1939), p. 289.

[14]Philip Van Doren Stern, The Annotated Walden (New
York: Clarkson and Potter, Inc., 1970), p. 43.

more than enough, lasting for five years, when it finally
went out of print until 1862.[15]

According to Canby, although America eventually rele-
gated Walden "to the humble position of accessory reading
about nature," it "picked up admirers, one by one, all
over the world" and eventually "won its place as a world
classic of literature" (p. 293). George Eliot's long review, with excerpts from Walden, in the Westminster Review
in London in 1856, indicates the beginning of this bit-by-
bit European trend. She says that Walden is "quite interesting enough" for her to break the magazine's rule against
"retrospective" reviewing. The book shows "a refined as
well as a hardy mind" and contains "plenty of sturdy sense":

> . . . we have a bit of pure American life (not the
> "go ahead" species, but its opposite pole), animated
> by that energetic, yet calm spirit of innovation, that
> practical as well as theoretic independence of formu-
> lae, which is peculiar to some of the finer American
> minds.[16]

Quotation Shifting from Summary to Full Passage, Set Off.

Recognition was on its way, but in America it was long in
coming.

Walt Whitman's Leaves of Grass (1855) has a different
history from the other three classics of the 1850's. Although it was received in almost total silence, Leaves of
Grass, with a one-by-one gaining of readers, started its
very slow uphill climb about two weeks after publication,

---

[15]Stern, p. 41.

[16]"Contemporary Literature," Westminster Review, January 1856, p. 166. This unsigned article is identified as
George Eliot's by Stern's reference to it (p. 41).

Article in Periodical, with Explanation

mostly through Whitman's own efforts in distributing gift-copies and advertising himself. Hawthorne, Melville, and Thoreau were already known as authors before their new "classics" appeared. Whitman, though active as a journalist and newspaper editor, was totally unknown. Leaves of Grass was his first book. He financed it himself, but the first edition of 1,000 (July 6, 1855) was a total failure. Gay Wilson Allen estimates that it had as few as two or three dozen readers.[17] According to Allen, Whitman himself said in old age that not a single copy had sold, contradicting an early boast that it "sold readily" (loc. cit.). Certainly, Whitman and his publisher gave most of the 1,000 copies to reviewers, who failed to review, or to influential people and acquaintances.

One of these was Ralph Waldo Emerson, then America's leading man of letters. He had never heard of Whitman, but the letter he wrote thanking Whitman for his gift-copy was eventually to bring Leaves of Grass to public attention. Emerson wrote that he felt like coming to Brooklyn immediately to meet "my benefactor," calling the book "the most extraordinary piece of wit and wisdom that America has yet contributed."[18] But this was a private letter. Only one review--in the influential New York Tribune, July 23, 1855--

[17]The Solitary Singer: A Critical Biography of Walt Whitman (New York: The Macmillan Co., 1955), p. 150.

[18]Richard Rupp, Critics on Whitman (Coral Gables, Florida: University of Miami Press, 1972), p. 14.

broke the public silence until Whitman himself, apparently despairing, wrote three anonymous reviews in September. These seem to have stirred Putnam's Magazine to review the book as "a mixture of Yankee transcendentalism and New York rowdyism." Conceding a certain "original perception of nature, a manly brawn, and epic directness," the reviewer nevertheless found Whitman's mixed vocabulary making some passages "downright laughable."[19]

Next year (1856), Whitman financed a second edition, and advertised it in the Tribune by publishing Emerson's letter without his permission, which Emerson thought "a strange rude thing to do."[20] But the reaction was now hostile. Whittier is said to have thrown his gift-copy into the fire, perhaps because it contained a clipping of Emerson's letter, which Whitman had pasted into a number of his gifts (loc. cit.). Boston's Christian Examiner called the book "impious libidinousness"; the Criterion wrote:

> . . . it is impossible to imagine how a man's fancy could conceive such a mass of stupid filth, unless he were possessed of the soul of a sentimental donkey that had died of disappointed love. (loc. cit.)

Ellipsis at Beginning of Set-Off Quotation

The second edition, like the first, failed to sell, and the third (1860) failed also when the publisher went bankrupt at the outbreak of the Civil War.[21]

Nevertheless, Whitman was gaining readers one by one.

[19]Allen, p. 173.

[20]Allen, p. 174.

[21]Allen, "Walt Whitman," Encyclopaedia Britannica (1967).

Emerson continued to recommend <u>Leaves</u> <u>of</u> <u>Grass</u> to his friends, in spite of Whitman's "strange rude" publishing of his letter. Thoreau, to whom Whitman had sent a gift of the second edition, found it "exhilarating, encouraging," writing a friend that "it has done me more good than any reading for a long time," though he disliked its sensuality.[22] Out in Springfield, Illinois, in the law offices of Lincoln and Herndon, some law students began to discuss the newly-published <u>Leaves</u> <u>of</u> <u>Grass</u>, which William Herndon had put on the office table. One of the students wrote that Lincoln, "who during the criticisms had been apparently in the unapproachable depths of one of his glum moods of meditative silence," picked up the book and read it for over an hour, then turned back to the beginning, "and to our general surprise, began to read aloud," revealing "a charm of new life" in Whitman's poem. He praised its "vitality, freshness, unconventional sentiments, and unique form of expression, and claimed that Whitman gave promise of a new school of poetry." Lincoln took the book home that night, but returned it to the office table next day, saying that he had saved it "from being purified by fire by the women, and asked that it be kept there, where he often picked it up and read it aloud."[23]

Whitman kept expanding the poem, bringing out unsuccessful editions, and publicizing both it and himself. By June

[22]Rupp, p. 15.

[23]Allen, <u>Singer</u>, pp. 175-176.

Long Quotation Summarized

Short Title, When Author Has Several Works Cited

30, 1865, the book had become notorious for being "full of in-
decent passages," as the Secretary of the Interior, James Har-
lan, said on firing Whitman, then a government clerk, when he
discovered his authorship.[24] In 1881, the Attorney General of
Massachusetts threatened a Boston publisher with prosecution
for obscenity unless he withdrew some sections in the seventh
edition. Whitman shifted to Philadelphia, and, at last, with
the new publicity, Leaves of Grass began to make money and to
get the wide attention it holds to this day.[25]

None of these great classics, then, was a best seller in *Thesis*
its day. Though The Scarlet Letter made Hawthorne instantly *Restated*
famous, and though Moby-Dick received favorable reviews at
first, both went into early eclipse, with Moby-Dick almost
totally forgotten, or misunderstood, until well into the
twentieth century. America more or less overlooked Thoreau,
and Whitman met almost total silence, broken only by his own
efforts to advertise himself. Nevertheless, one thing seems
clear: from the first, with each of these American classics,
some readers, however few, recognized their greatness. Although The Scarlet Letter and Moby-Dick quietly faded, and *Clincher*
Leaves of Grass failed from the beginning, someone, somewhere,
read them, remembered them, and recommended them to others,
until they became generally recognized as the classics they
are.

[24]Allen, Walt Whitman Handbook (Chicago: Packard and
Co., 1946), p. 5.

[25]Allen, Encyc. Brit.

BIBLIOGRAPHY

Article   Allen, Gay Wilson. "Walt Whitman," Encyclopaedia Britannica (1967).

Books by
Same   _____. Walt Whitman Handbook. Chicago: Packard and
Author   Co., 1946.

_____. The Solitary Singer: A Critical Biography of
Walt Whitman. New York: The Macmillan Co., 1955.

Two Cities of   Branch, Watson G. Melville: The Critical Heritage. Lon-
Publication   don and Boston: Routlege & Kegan Paul, 1947.

Canby, Henry Seidel. Thoreau. Boston: Houghton Mifflin
Co., 1939.

Author   [Eliot, George.] "Contemporary Literature," Westminster
Anonymous   Review, January, 1856, pp. 124-172.
on Publication

Hawthorne, Julian. Hawthorne and His Circle. New York:
Harper & Brothers, 1903.

Hetherington, Hugh W. Melville's Reviewers, British and
American, 1846-1891. Chapel Hill: University of North
Carolina Press, 1961.

James, Henry. Hawthorne. Ithaca: Cornell University
Press, 1967.

Further   Rupp, Richard. Critics on Whitman. Coral Gables, Florida:
Identification   University of Miami Press, 1972.
for City of
Publication   Stern, Philip Van Doren. The Annotated Walden. New York:
Clarkson and Potter, Inc., 1970.

Stewart, Randall. Nathaniel Hawthorne: A Biography. New
Haven: Yale University Press, 1948.

Introduction   Stowe, Harriet Beecher. "The Author's Introduction," Uncle
in Book   Tom's Cabin, or, Life Among the Lowly. Boston and New
York: Houghton Mifflin and Co., 1896. Pp. liii-xc.

EXERCISES

1 Consult the current *World Almanac and Book of Facts* for the date of some memorable event; the sinking of the *Titanic* or the *Lusitania,* Lindbergh's flight over the Atlantic, the United States' entry into war, the founding of the United Nations, the great stock-market crash, or the like. Now go to another collection, like *Facts on File,* and some of the other almanacs and yearbooks for the year of your event; write an essay entitled, let us say, "1929" — a synopsis of the monumental and the quaint for that year, as lively and interesting as you can make it.

2 Look up some event of the recent past (after 1913) in the *New York Times Index*. Write a paper on how the event is reported in the *Times* and in the other newspapers available in your library.

3 Select some well-known literary work: *Walden, David Copperfield, Huckleberry Finn, Alice in Wonderland, The Wind in the Willows, A Farewell to Arms*. Describe how thoroughly it is cataloged by your library. Check cards for author, title, and subject. How many editions does the library have? Is the work contained within any *Works?* How many cards treat it as a subject? Does your library own a first edition? This last may require that you find the date of the first edition by looking up your author in an encyclopedia, checking available books about him, and perhaps checking in the British Museum's *General Catalogue of Printed Books,* or, for a twentieth-century book, *United States Catalog of Printed Books* or *Cumulative Book Index* to discover the earliest cataloging.

4 Choose a subject like the origin of man, Watergate (or a similar affair), *apartheid* — anything that interests you — and compile a bibliographical list of the articles given in the *Reader's Guide,* beginning with the most recent issue and going backward in time until you have eight or ten titles. You may have to look under several headings, such as "archeology," "anthropology," and "evolution," for the origin of man; under "U.S. Government" and others in addition to "Watergate" itself for the Watergate affair; and under "South Africa," "racism," and "apartheid" itself for *apartheid*. Then look in the scholarly *Indexes* discussed on p. 91; make another bibliographical listing of your subject for the same period. Which articles appear in the *Humanities* or *Social Science Index* (or both) only? Which articles appear in the *Reader's Guide* only? Which appear in both the *Indexes* and the *Guide?* Write a brief commentary about the differences in coverage in these two (or three) indexes. What does comparing them tell you about research?

5 In the *Essay and General Literature Index,* look up three essays published in anthologies between 1965 and 1969 on Gerard Manley Hopkins, recording each entry and then following it by full data on the book, with call number, from the card catalog.

A Handbook A
Writer's Grammar

You have already seen, in preceding chapters, many of the ills of writing—the ailing thesis that weakens the whole system, the *of*-and-*which* disease, the recurring rashes of wordiness. But many a sentence suffers from ailments more deeply genetic. You can probably tell when a sentence feels bad, especially after your instructor has marked it up. You can, in other words, detect the symptoms, but to work an efficient cure you need also to find the causes and to treat them directly. You need some skill in the ancient remedies of grammar.

THE BASIC PARTS OF SPEECH

The parts of speech are the elements of the sentence. A grasp of the basic eight—nouns, pronouns, verbs, adjectives, adverbs, prepositions, conjunctions, and interjections—will give you a sense of the whole.

NOUNS. Nouns name something. A *proper noun* names a particular person, place, or thing. A *common noun* names a general class of things; a common noun naming a group as a single unit is a *collective noun*. A phrase or clause functioning as a noun is a *noun phrase* or a *noun clause*. Here are some examples:

COMMON: stone, tree, house, girl, artist, nation, democracy
PROPER: George, Cincinnati, Texas, Europe, Declaration of Independence
COLLECTIVE: committee, family, quartet, herd, navy, clergy, kind
NOUN PHRASE: *Riding the surf* takes stamina.
NOUN CLAUSE: *What you say* may depend on *how you say it.*

PRONOUNS. As their name indicates, pronouns stand "for nouns." The noun a pronoun represents is called its *antecedent.* Pronouns show *case*—nominative *(I, we, he, she, they),* possessive *(my, our, his, her, their),* and objective *(me, us, him, her, them).* Pronouns may be classified as follows:

PERSONAL *(standing for persons):* I, you, he, she, we, they; me, him, her, us, them; my, his, our, and so on
REFLEXIVE *(turning the action back on the doer):* I hurt *myself.* They enjoy *themselves. (himself, herself, itself)*
INTENSIVE *(emphasizing the doer):* He *himself* said so.
RELATIVE *(linking subordinate clauses):* who, which, that, whose, whomever, whichever, and so on
INTERROGATIVE *(beginning a question):* who, which, what
DEMONSTRATIVE *(pointing to persons or things):* this, that, these, those, such
INDEFINITE *(standing for indefinite numbers of persons or things):* any, each, few, some, anyone, no one, everyone, somebody, and so on
RECIPROCAL *(plural reflexives):* each other, one another

Note that pronouns describing nouns function as adjectives:

PRONOUNS: *Few* would recognize *this.*
PRONOUNS AS ADJECTIVES: *Few* readers would recognize *this* allusion.

VERBS. Verbs express actions or states of being. A verb may be *transitive,* requiring an object to complete the thought, or *intransitive,* requiring no object for completeness. Some verbs can function either transitively or intransitively. *Linking verbs* link the subject to a state of being.

TRANSITIVE: He *put* his feet on the chair. She *hit* the ceiling. They *sang* a sad old song.
INTRANSITIVE: He *smiled.* She *cried.* They *sang* like birds. They *are coming.*
LINKING: He *is* happy. She *feels* angry. This *looks* bad. It *is* she.

ADJECTIVES. Adjectives describe, or modify, nouns or pronouns. An *adjectival phrase* or *adjectival clause* functions in a sentence as a single adjective would.

> ADJECTIVES: The *red* house faces west. He was a *handsome* devil. The *old haunted* house was *empty. These* books belong to *that* student.
> ADJECTIVAL PHRASE: He had reached the end *of the book.*
> ADJECTIVAL CLAUSE: Here is the key *that unlocks the barn.*

Articles, which point out nouns, are classified with adjectives. *The,* the "definite" article, points to specific persons or things; *A* and *an,* the "indefinite" articles, point out persons or things as members of groups.

> ARTICLES: *The* hunter selected *a* rifle from *an* assortment.

ADVERBS. Adverbs describe verbs, adjectives, or other adverbs, completing the ideas of *how, how much, when,* and *where.* An *adverbial phrase* or *adverbial clause* functions as a single adverb would.

> ADVERBS: Though *slightly* fat, he runs *quickly* and plays *extremely well.*
> ADVERBIAL PHRASE: He left *after the others.*
> ADVERBIAL CLAUSE: She lost the gloves *after she left the store.*

PREPOSITIONS. A preposition links a noun or pronoun to another word in the sentence. A preposition and its object form a *prepositional phrase,* which acts as an adjective or adverb:

> The repairman opened the base OF *the telephone.* [adjective, modifies *base*]
> BY *late afternoon,* Williams was exhausted. [adverb, modifies *was*]
> He walked TO *his car* and drove FROM *the field.* [adverbs, modify *walked* and *drove*]

Certain forms of verbs, alone or in phrases, serve as nouns, adjectives, and adverbs. *Participles* act as adjectives. *Present participles* are verbs plus *-ing,* and *past participles* are regular verbs plus *-ed* (see the Glossary of Usage for *Irregular verbs*). *Gerunds,* like present participles, are verbs plus *-ing* but work as nouns; past participles occasionally function as nouns, also. *Infinitives, to* plus verbs, serve as nouns, adjectives, or adverbs. Unlike participles and gerunds, infinitives can have subjects, which are always in the objective case.

> PRESENT PARTICIPLES: *Feeling miserable* and *running a fever,* she took to her bed. [adjectives]

PAST PARTICIPLES: The nurses treated the *wounded* soldier. [adjective]

The nurses treated the *wounded.* [noun]

GERUND PHRASE: *His going* ended the friendship. [noun, subject of sentence]

INFINITIVES: *To err* is human; *to forgive,* divine. [nouns, subjects of sentence]

I saw *him* [*to*] *go.* [phrase serving as noun, object of *saw*; *him* subject of *to go*]

Ford is the man *to watch.* [adjective]

Coiled, the snake waited *to strike.* [adverb]

CONJUNCTIONS. Conjunctions join words, phrases, and clauses. *Coordinating* conjunctions—*and, but, or, yet*—join equals:

Mary *and* I won easily.

Near the shore *but* far from home, the bottle floated.

He was talented, *yet* he failed.

Subordinating conjunctions attach clauses to the basic subject-and-verb:

Since it was late, they left.

He worked hard *because* he needed an A.

They stopped *after* they reached the spring.

INTERJECTIONS. Interjections interrupt the usual flow of the sentence to emphasize feelings:

But, *oh,* the difference to me.

Mr. Dowd, *alas,* has ignored the evidence.

The consumer will suddenly discover that, *ouch,* his dollar is cut in half.

AGREEMENT: NOUNS AND VERBS

Make your verb and its subject agree.

Match singulars with singulars, plurals with plurals. First find the verb, since that names the action—*sways* in the following sentence: "The poplar tree sways in the wind, dropping yellow leaves on the lawn." Then ask *who* or *what* sways, and you have your simple subject: *tree,* a singular noun. Then make sure that your singular subject matches its singular verb. (A reminder: contrary to nouns, the majority of singular verbs end in *s—actors perform; the actor performs.*) You will have little trouble except when subject and verb are far apart, or when the number of the subject itself is doubtful. (Is *family* singular or plural? What about *none?* What about *neither he nor she?*)

> FAULTY: *Revision* of their views about markets and averages *are* mandatory.
> REVISED: **Revision of their views about markets and averages** *is* **mandatory.**

Sidestep the plural constructions that fall between your singular subject and its verb:

> FAULTY: **The** *attention* **of the students** *wander* **out the window.**
> REVISED: **The** *attention* **of the students** *wanders* **out the window.**

> FAULTY: **The** *plaster,* **as well as the floors,** *need* **repair.**
> REVISED: **The** *plaster,* **as well as the floors,** *needs* **repair.**

Collective nouns *(committee, jury, herd, group, family, kind, quartet)* are single units (plural in British usage); give them singular verbs, or plural members:

> FAULTY: **Her** *family were* **ready.**
> REVISED: **Her** *family was* **ready.**

> FAULTY: **The** *jury have disagreed* **among themselves.**
> REVISED: **The** *jurors have disagreed* **among themselves.**

> FAULTY: **These** *kind* **of muffins** *are* **delicious.**
> REVISED: *These muffins are* **delicious.**
> REVISED: *This kind* **of muffin** *is* **delicious.**

Watch out for the indefinite pronouns—*each, neither, anyone, everyone, no one, none, everybody, nobody.* Each of these is (not *are*) singular in idea, yet each flirts with the crowd from which it singles out its idea: each of *these,* either of *them,* none of *them.* Give all of them singular verbs.

> *None* **of these men** *is* **a failure.**
> *None* **of the class, even the best prepared,** *wants* **the test.**
> *Everybody,* **including the high-school kids,** *goes* **to Andy's Drive-In.**
> *Neither* **the right nor the left** *supports* **the issue.**

None of them are is very common. From Shakespeare's time to ours, it has persisted alongside the more precise *none of them is,* which seems to have the edge in careful prose.

When one side of the *either-or* contrast is plural, you have a problem, conventionally solved by matching the verb to the nearer noun:

Either the players or the coach *is* bad.

Since *players is* disturbs some feelings for plurality, the best solution is probably to switch your nouns:

Either the coach or the players *are* bad.

When both sides of the contrast are plural, the verb is naturally also plural:

Neither the rights of man nor the needs of the commonwealth *are* relevant to the question.

Don't let a plural noun in the predicate lure you into a plural verb:

FAULTY: **His most faithful rooting *section are* his family and his girl.**
REVISED: **His most faithful rooting *section is* his family and his girl.**
REVISED: **His family and his girl *are* his best rooting section.**

ALIGNING THE VERBS

Verbs have *tense* (past, present, future), *mood* (indicative, imperative, subjunctive), and *voice* (active, passive). These can sometimes slip out of line, as your thought slips, so a review should be useful here:

Use the tense that best expresses your idea.

Each tense (from Latin *tempus,* meaning time) has its own virtues for expressing what you want your sentences to say. Use the *present tense,* of course, to express present action: "Now she *knows.* She *is leaving.*" Use the present also for habitual action: "He *sees* her every day," and for describing literary events: "Hamlet *finds* the king praying, but he *is* unable to act; he *lets* the opportunity slip." And use the present tense to express timeless facts: "The Greeks knew the world *is* round." Otherwise, apply the *past tense* to all action before the present:

One day I *was watching* television when the phone *rang;* it *was* the police.
In the center of the cracked facade, the door *sagged;* rubble *lay* all around the foundations.

Use the *future tense* for action expected after the present:

> He *will finish* it next year.
> When he *finishes* next year, ... [The present functioning as future]
> He *is going to finish* it next year. [The "present progressive" *is going* plus an infinitive, like *to finish,* commonly expresses the future.]

Use the *present perfect tense* for action completed ("perfected") but relevant to the present moment:

> I *have gone* there before.
> He *has sung* forty concerts.
> She *has driven* there every day.

Use the *past perfect tense* to express "the past of the past":

> "When we *arrived* [past], they *had finished* [past perfect]."

Similarly, use the *future perfect tense* to express "the past of the future":

> When we *arrive* [future], they *will have finished* [future perfect].
> You *will have worked* thirty hours by Christmas. [future perfect].
> The flare *will signal* [future] that he *has started* [perfect].

Set your tense, then move your reader clearly forward or back from it as your thought requires:

> Hamlet *finds* the king praying. He *had sworn* instant revenge the night before, but he *will achieve* it only by accident and about a week later. Here he *is* unable to act; he *loses* his best opportunity.

But avoid mixtures like this: "Hamlet *finds* the king praying, but he *was* unable to act; he *let* the opportunity slip." Here, all the verbs should be in the present, corresponding to *finds*.

Keep your moods in mind.

The *indicative mood*, which indicates matters of fact (our usual verb and way of writing), and the *imperative mood*, which commands ("Do this," "Keep your moods in mind"), will give you no trouble. The *subjunctive mood*, which expresses an action or condition not asserted as actual fact, occasionally will. The conditional, provisional, wishful, suppositional ideas expressed by the subjunctive are usually subjoined (*subjunctus*, "yoked under") in subordinate clauses. The form of the verb is often plural, even though the subject is singular.

He looked as if he *were* confident.
If I *were* you, Miles, I would ask her myself.
If this *be* error, and upon me [*be*] proved . . . .
Had he *been* sure, he would have said so.
I demand that he *make* restitution.
I move that the nominations *be closed,* and that the secretary *cast* a
   unanimous ballot.

Don't mix active and passive voice.
One parting shot at our friend the passive. Avoid misaligning
active with passive in the same sentence:

As he *entered* the room, voices *were heard* [he *heard*].
After they *laid out* the pattern, electric shears *were used* [they *used*
   electric shears].

You can also think of this as an awkward shift of subject, from *he* to
voices, from *they* to *shears.* Here is a slippery sample, where the subject stays the same:

FAULTY: This plan *reduces* taxes and *has been used* successfully in
   three other cities.
REVISED: This plan *reduces* taxes and *has been* successful in three
   other cities.
REVISED: This plan *reduces* taxes and *has proved* workable in three
   other cities.

REFERENCE OF PRONOUNS

Match your pronouns to what they stand for.
Pronouns stand for (*pro*) nouns. They *refer* back to nouns already
expressed (*antecedents*), or they stand for conceptions (people,
things, ideas) already established or implied, as in *"None* of *them* is
perfect."* Pronouns must agree with the singular and plural ideas
they represent.
When a relative pronoun (*who, which, that*) is the subject of a
clause, it takes a singular verb if its antecedent is singular, a plural
verb is its antecedent is plural:

Phil is the only *one* of our swimmers WHO *has* won three gold
   medals. [The antecedent is *one,* not *swimmers.*]
Phil is one of the best *swimmers* WHO *have* ever been on the team.
   [The antecedent is *swimmers,* not *one.*]

Pronouns may stand either as subjects or objects of the action, and their form changes accordingly.

Use nominative pronouns for nominative functions.

Those pronouns in the predicate that refer back to the subject are troublesome; keep them nominative:

> He discovered that it was *I*.
> It was *they* who signed the treaty.

Another example is that of the pronoun in *apposition* with the subject (that is, *positioned near,* and meaning the same thing as, the subject):

> *We* students would rather talk than sleep.

After *than* and *as,* the pronoun is usually the subject of an implied verb:

> She is taller than *I* [am].
> You are as bright as *he* [is].
> She loves you as much as *I* [do].

But note: "She loves you as much as [she loves] *me.*" Match your pronouns to what they stand for, subjects for subjects, objects for objects. (But a caution: Use an objective pronoun as the subject of an infinitive. See p. 125.)

Use a nominative pronoun as subject of a noun clause. This is the trickiest of pronominal problems, because the subject of the clause also looks like the object of the main verb:

> FAULTY: The sergeant asked *whomever* did it to step forward.
> REVISED: The sergeant asked *whoever* did it to step forward.

Similarly, parenthetical remarks like *I think, he says,* and *we believe* often make pronouns seem objects when they are actually subjects:

> FAULTY: Ellen is the girl *whom* I think *will succeed.*
> REVISED: Ellen is the girl *who* I think *will succeed.*

Use objective pronouns for objective functions.

Compound objects give most of the trouble. Try the pronoun by itself: "invited *me*," "sent *him*," and so forth. These are all correct:

> The mayor invited my wife and *me* to dinner. [*not* my wife and *I*]
> Between *her* and *me,* an understanding grew.

They sent it to Stuart and *him.*
. . . for you and *me.*
He would not think of letting *us* girls help him.

Use a possessive pronoun before a gerund.
Since gerunds are *-ing* words used as nouns, the pronouns attached to them must say what they mean:

FAULTY: She disliked *him* hunting.
REVISED: She disliked *his* hunting.

The object of her dislike is not *him* but *hunting.*

Keep your antecedents clear.
If an antecedent is missing, ambiguous, vague, or remote, the pronoun will suffer from "faulty reference."

MISSING: In Texas *they* produce a lot of oil.
REVISED: Texas produces a lot of oil.

AMBIGUOUS: Paul smashed into a girl's *car who* was visiting his sister.
REVISED: Paul smashed into the car of a *girl* visiting his sister.

VAGUE: Because Ann had never spoken before an audience, she was afraid of *it.*
REVISED: Because Ann had never spoken before an audience, she was afraid.

REMOTE: The castle was built in 1537. The rooms and furnishings are carefully kept up, but the entrance is now guarded by a coin-fed turnstile. *It* still belongs to the Earl.
REVISED: The castle, which still belongs to the Earl, was built in 1537. The rooms and furnishings are carefully kept up, but the entrance is now guarded by a coin-fed turnstile.

This poses a special problem, especially when heading a sentence ("This is a special problem"). Many good stylists insist that every *this* refer back to a specific noun—*report* in the following example:

The commission submitted its *report. This* proved windy, evasive, and ineffectual.

Others occasionally allow (as I do) a more colloquial *this,* referring back more broadly:

The commission submitted its report. This ended the matter.

Give an indefinite or general antecedent a singular pronoun.

FAULTY: *Each* of the students hoped to follow in *their* teacher's footsteps.

REVISED: *Each* of the students hoped to follow in *his* [or *his or her*] teacher's footsteps.

REVISED: *All* of the students hoped to follow in *their* teacher's footsteps. [Here, we have a single class.]

FAULTY: If the *government* dares to face the new philosophy, *they* should declare *themselves.*

REVISED: If the *government* dares to face the new philosophy, *it* should declare *itself.*

Keep person and number consistent.

Don't slip from person to person (*I* to *they*); don't fall among singulars and plurals — or you will get bad references.

FAULTY: *They* have reached an age when *you* should know better.

REVISED: *They* have reached an age when *they* should know better.

FAULTY: A motion *picture* can improve upon a book, but *they* usually do not.

REVISED: A motion *picture* can improve upon a book, but *it* usually does not.

MODIFIERS MISUSED AND MISPLACED

Keep your adjectives and adverbs straight.

The adjective sometimes wrongly crowds out the adverb: "He played a *real* conservative game." And the adverb sometimes steals the adjective's place, especially when the linking verb looks transitive but isn't (*feels, looks, tastes, smells*), making the sense wrong: "He feels *badly*" (adverb) means incompetence, not misery. The cure is in modifying your nouns with adjectives, and modifying everything else with adverbs:

He played a *really* conservative game. [adverb]
He feels *bad.* [adjective]
This tastes *good.* [adjective]
I feel *good.* [adjective — spirit]
I feel *well.* [adjective — health]
This works *well.* [adverb]

Some words serve both as adjectives and adverbs: *early, late, near, far, hard, only, little, right, wrong, straight, well, better, best, fast,* for example. These words are linguistic windfalls, to be squeezed for their juice:

> Think *little* of *little* things.

Near is a hard case, serving as an adjective (*the near future*) and as an adverb of place (*near the barn*), and then also trying to serve for *nearly,* the adverb of degree:

> FAULTY: We are nowhere *near* knowledgeable enough.
> REVISED: We are not *nearly* knowledgeable enough.
>
> FAULTY: It was a *near* treasonous statement.
> REVISED: It was a *nearly* treasonous statement.
>
> FAULTY: With Dodge, he has a tie of *near*-filial rapport.
> REVISED: With Dodge, he has an *almost* filial rapport.

Slow has a long history as an adverb, but *slowly* keeps the upper hand in print. Notice that adverbs usually go after, and adjectives before:

> The *slow* freight went *slowly*.

Make your comparisons complete.

Ask yourself "Than what?"—when you find your sentences ending with a *greener* (adjective) or a *more smoothly* (adverb):

> FAULTY: The western plains are *flatter.*
> REVISED: The western plains are *flatter than* those east of the Mississippi.
>
> FAULTY: He plays more *skillfully.*
> REVISED: He plays more *skillfully than* most boys his age.
>
> FAULTY: Jane told her more than Ellen.
> REVISED: Jane told her more than she told Ellen.
>
> FAULTY: His income is lower than a *busboy.*
> REVISED: His income is lower than a *busboy's.*

Don't let your modifiers squint.

Some modifiers squint in two directions at once. Place them to modify one thing only.

> FAULTY: They agreed *when both sides ceased fire* to open negotiations.
> REVISED: They agreed to open negotiations *when both sides ceased fire.*

FAULTY: Several delegations *we know* have failed.
REVISED: *We know* that several delegations have failed.

FAULTY: They hoped to try *thoroughly* to understand.
REVISED: They hoped to try to understand *thoroughly*.

FAULTY: He resolved to dependably develop plans.
REVISED: He resolved to develop dependable plans.

Don't let your modifers or references dangle.

The *-ing* words (the gerunds and participles) tend to slip loose from the sentence and dangle, referring to nothing or the wrong thing.

FAULTY: Going home, the walk was slippery. [participle]
REVISED: Going home, I found the walk slippery.

FAULTY: When getting out of bed, his toe hit the dresser. [gerund]
REVISED: When getting out of bed, he hit his toe on the dresser.

Infinitive phrases also can dangle badly:

FAULTY: To think clearly, some logic is important.
REVISED: To think clearly, you should learn some logic.

Any phrase or clause may dangle:

FAULTY: When only a freshman [phrase], Jim's history teacher inspired him.
REVISED: When Jim was only a freshman, his history teacher inspired him.

FAULTY: After he had taught thirty years [clause], the average student still seemed average.
REVISED: After he had taught thirty years, he found the average student still average.

FRAGMENTS, COMMA SPLICES, AND RUN-ONS

Align your thoughts as complete sentences.

As you have seen, the fragment—any piece of a sentence, with subject or predicate missing—may have superb rhetorical force: "So what." But when fragments slip in unnoticed, they reveal a failure to grasp the sentence completely. You have lost the fundamental connection between subject and verb, and the parts related to them.

FAULTY: He does not spell everything out. But rather hints that something is wrong, and leaves the rest up to the reader.

REVISED: He does not *spell* everything out, but rather *hints* . . . , and *leaves* . . . [subject with compound verb, set off by commas]

FAULTY: Yet here is her husband treating their son to all that she considers evil. Plus the fact that the boy is offered beer.

REVISED: Yet here is her husband treating their son to all that she considers evil, especially beer.

FAULTY: He points out that one never knows what the future will bring. Because it is actually a matter of luck.

REVISED: He points out that one never knows what the future will bring, because it is actually a matter of luck. [dependent clause now properly connected]

With run-ons—two sentences shuffled together as one—the grammatical grip is even more feeble than with the fragment. Somehow the writer has never grasped the sentence as a discrete marriage of subject and verb. All kinds of parties just stumble in together:

FAULTY: He went to class, he forgot his paper. [comma splice]
FAULTY: He went to class he forgot his paper. [run-on sentence]
REVISED: (a) He went to class. He forgot his paper.
    (b) He went to class; he forgot his paper.
    (c) He went to class, but he forgot his paper.
    (d) When he got to class, he found that he had forgotten his paper.

Conjunctive adverbs (*however, therefore, nevertheless, moreover, furthermore,* and others) may cause trouble.

FAULTY: She continued teaching, however her heart was not in it.
REVISED: (a) She continued teaching, but her heart was not in it.
    (b) She continued teaching; however, her heart was not in it.
    (c) She continued teaching; her heart, however, was not in it.

Similarly, transitional phrases (*in fact, that is, for example*) may run your sentences together:

FAULTY: He disliked discipline, that is, he really was lazy.
REVISED: (a) He disliked discipline; that is, he really was lazy.
    (b) He disliked discipline, that is, anything demanding.

EXERCISES

1 Straighten out these disagreements and misalignments.

1. These kind of questions are sheer absurdities.
2. Conservatism, as well as liberalism, are summonses for change in American life as we know it.
3. Neither the fringe on his jacket nor the price of his guitar impress us.
4. Her family were bitter about it.
5. The grazing ground of both the antelope and the wild horses are west of this range.
6. The campus, as well as the town, need to wake up.
7. The extinction of several species of whales are threatened.
8. None of the group, even Smith and Jones, want to play.
9. Holden goes to New York. He looked up his old teacher and called his old girl friend. Before he started, he had decided to call his sister, but actually he took almost the whole book to get around to calling her. In the end, she proved to be his best friend.
10. If I would have studied harder, I would have passed.
11. They insisted that he shows up.
12. The sit-in accomplished its purpose and was tested by fire.
13. First he investigated the practical implications, and then the moral implications that were involved were examined.

2 Revise these faulty pronouns, and their sentences where necessary.

1. None of us are perfect.
2. Doug is the only one of the boys who always stand straight.
3. We are stronger than them.
4. He took my wife and I to dinner.
5. Jim will vote for whomever they say is a winner.
6. He opened the bird's cage, and it flew away.
7. It was him all right.
8. She disliked him whistling the same old tune.
9. He will give the ticket to whomever wants it: he did it for you and I.
10. My mother insists on me buying my own clothes: the average girl likes their independence.
11. The buffalo is far from extinct. Their numbers are actually increasing.

12. The program was turned into a fiasco by bad planning. This was bad.

3 Straighten out these adjectives and adverbs:

1. The demonstration reached near riot proportions.
2. It smells awfully.
3. The dress fitted her perfect.
4. He has a reasonable good chance.
5. His car had a special built engine.

4 Complete and adjust these partial thoughts:

1. He swims more smoothly.
2. The pack of a paratrooper is lighter than a soldier.
3. The work of a student is more intense than his parents.
4. This is the best painting.
5. The moon is smaller.

5 Unsquint these modifiers:

1. She planned on the next day to call him.
2. They asked after ten days to be notified.
3. The party promised to completely attempt reform.
4. Several expeditions we know have failed.
5. We wanted to win enough to cry.

ϩ Mend these danglers:

1. What we need is a file of engineers broken down by their specialties.
2. Following the games on television, the batting average of every player was at his fingertips.
3. When entering the room, the lamp fell over.
4. To study well, a quiet room helps.
5. After he arrived at the dorm, his father phoned.

7 Correct the following:

1. He left his second novel unfinished. Perhaps because of his basic uncertainty, which he never overcame.
2. He entered the race for the presidency. Knowing all along that he could not win.
3. He seems to play a careless game. But actually knows exactly what he is doing, and intends to put his opponent off guard.

4. He played to win, that is, he gave every game all he had.

5. His idea of democracy was incomplete, he himself had slaves.

8 Cure the following grammatical ailments:

1. The professor as well as the students were glad the course was over.

2. We study hard at State, but you do not have to work all the time.

3. Holden goes to New York and learned about life.

4. As he looked up, a light could be seen in the window.

5. A citizen should support the government, but they should also be free to criticize it.

6. It will all come true, for you and I.

7. The students always elect whomever is popular.

8. She hated me leaving so early.

9. This is one of the best essays that has been submitted.

10. While playing the piano, the dog sat by me and howled.

11. The team had a near perfect record.

12. Run-on sentences show a failure deeper than fragments.

Handbook B
Punctuation, Spelling, Capitalization

Punctuation gives the silent page some of the breath of life. It marks the pauses and emphases with which a speaker points his meaning. Loose punctuators forget what every good writer knows: that even silent reading produces an articulate murmur in our heads, that language springs from the breathing human voice, that the beauty and meaning of language depend on what the written word makes us *hear*, on the sentence's tuning of emphasis and pause. Commas, semicolons, colons, periods, and other punctuation transcribe our meaningful pauses to the printed page.

THE PERIOD: MARKING THE SENTENCE

A period marks a sentence, a subject completed in its verb:

She walked.

A phrase — which lacks a verb, though it may contain a verb *form* (see p. 124) — subordinates this idea, making it *depend on* some other main clause:

While walking, **she thought.**

A subordinate clause does the same, making the whole original sentence subordinate:

While she walked, **she thought.**

Like a period, and a question mark, an exclamation mark marks a sentence, but much more emphatically: *Plan to revise!* Use it sparingly if you want it to count rhetorically.

Take special care not to break off a phrase or clause with a period, making a fragment that looks like a sentence but isn't (unless you intend a rhetorical fragment—see p. 56), and don't use the comma as a period (see p. 135).

FAULTY: **She dropped the cup. Which had cost twenty dollars.**
REVISED: **She dropped the cup, which had cost twenty dollars.**

FAULTY: **He swung furiously, the ball sailed into the lake.**
REVISED: **He swung furiously. The ball sailed into the lake.**

THE COMMA

Here are the four basic commas:

I. THE INTRODUCER—after introductory phrases and clauses.
II. THE COORDINATOR—between "sentences" joined by *and, but, or, nor, yet, so, for.*
III. THE INSERTER—a PAIR around any inserted word or phrase.
IV. THE LINKER—when adding other words or phrases.

I. THE INTRODUCER. A comma after every introductory word or phrase makes your writing clearer, more alive with the breath and pause of meaning:

Indeed, the idea failed.
After the first letter, she wrote again.
In the autumn of the same year, he went to Paris.

Without the introductory comma, your reader frequently expects something else:

After the first letter she wrote, she . . . .
In the autumn of the same year he went to Paris, he . . . .

But beware! What looks like an introductory phrase or clause may actually be the subject of the sentence *and should take no comma.* A comma can break up a good marriage of subject and verb. The comma in each of these is an interloper, and should be removed:

That handsome man in the ascot tie, is the groom.
The idea that you should report every observation, is wrong.
The realization that we must be slightly dishonest to be truly kind,
comes to all of us sooner or later.

If your clause-as-subject is unusually long, or confusing, you may relieve the pressure by inserting some qualifying remark after it, between two commas:

The idea that you should report every observation, *however insignificant,* **is wrong.**
The realization that we must be slightly dishonest to be truly kind,
obviously the higher motive, **comes to all of us sooner or later.**

II. THE COORDINATOR—between "sentences" joined by coordinate conjunctions. You will often see the comma omitted when your two clauses are short: "He hunted and she fished." But nothing is wrong with "He hunted, and she fished." The comma, in fact, shows the slight pause you make when you say it.

Think of the "comma-and" **(, and)** as a unit equivalent to the period. The period, the semicolon, and the "comma-and" **(, and)** all designate independent clauses—independent "sentences"—but give different emphases:

.   **He was tired. He went home.**
;   **He was tired; he went home.**
, and   **He was tired, and he went home.**

A comma tells your reader that another subject and predicate are coming:

He hunted the hills and dales.
He hunted the hills, and she fished in the streams.
She was naughty but nice.
She was naughty, but that is not our business.
Wear your jacket or coat.
Wear your jacket, or you will catch cold.
It was strong yet sweet.
It was strong, yet it was not unpleasant.

Of course, you may use a comma in *all* the examples above if your sense demands it. The contrasts set by *but, or,* and *yet* often urge a comma, and the even stronger contrasts with *not* and *either-or* demand a comma, whether or not full predication follows:

> It was strong, yet sweet.
> It was a battle, not a game.
> . . . a bird in the hand, or two in the bush.

Commas signal where you would pause in speaking.

The meaningful pause also urges an occasional comma in compound predicates, usually not separated by commas:

> He granted the usual permission and walked away.
> He granted the usual permission, and walked away.

Both are correct. In the first sentence, however, the granting and walking are perfectly routine, and the temper unruffled. In the second, some kind of emotion has forced a pause, and a comma, after *permission*. Similarly, meaning itself may demand a comma between the two verbs:

> He turned and dropped the vase.
> He turned, and dropped the vase.

In the first sentence, he turned the vase; in the second, himself. Your **, and** in compound predicates suggests some touch of drama, some meaningful distinction, or afterthought.

You need a comma before *for* and *still* even more urgently. Without the comma, their conjunctive meaning changes; they assume their ordinary roles, *for* as a preposition, *still* as an adjective or adverb:

> She liked him still . . . . [That is, either *yet* or *quiet!*]
> She liked him, still she could not marry him.
> She liked him for his money.
> She liked him, for a good man is hard to find.

An observation: *for* is the weakest of all the coordinators. Almost a subordinator, it is perilously close to *because*. *For* can seem moronic if cause and effect are fairly obvious: "She liked him, for he was kind." Either make a point of the cause by full subordination — "She liked him *because* he was kind" — or flatter the reader with a semicolon: "She liked him; he was kind." *For* is effective only when the cause is somewhat hard to find: "Blessed are the meek, for they shall inherit the earth."

To summarize the basic point about the comma as coordinator: put a comma before the coordinator (*and, but, or, nor, yet, so, still, for,*) when joining independent clauses, and add others necessary for emphasis or clarity.

III. THE INSERTER. Put a PAIR of commas around every inserted word, phrase, or clause—those expressions that seem parenthetical and are called "nonrestrictive." When you cut a sentence in two to insert something necessary, you need to tie off *both* ends, or your sentence will die on the table:

> When he packs his bag, however he goes. [, however,]
> The car, an ancient Packard is still running. [, an ancient Packard,]
> April 10, 1980 is agreeable as a date for final payment. [, 1980,]
> John Jones, Jr. is wrong. [, Jr.,]
> I wish, John you would do it. [, John,]

You do not mean that 1980 is agreeable, nor are you telling John Jones that Junior is wrong. Such parenthetical insertions need a *pair* of commas:

> The case, *nevertheless,* was closed.
> She will see, *if she has any sense at all,* that he is right.
> Sam, *on the other hand,* may be wrong.
> Note, *for example,* the excellent brushwork.
> John Jones, *M.D.,* and Bill Jones, *Ph.D.,* doctored the punch to perfection.
> He stopped at Kansas City, *Missouri,* for two hours.

The same rule applies to all *nonrestrictive* remarks, phrases, and clauses—all elements simply additive, explanatory, and hence parenthetical:

> John, *my friend,* will do what he can.
> Andy, *his project sunk, his hopes shattered,* was speechless.
> The taxes, *which are reasonable,* will be paid.
> That man, *who knows,* is not talking.

Think of *nonrestrictive* as "nonessential" to your meaning, hence set off by commas. Think of *restrictive* as essential and "restricting" your meaning, hence not set off at all (use *which* for nonrestrictives, *that* for restrictives; see p. 65):

RESTRICTIVES:
> The taxes that are reasonable will be paid.
> Southpaws who are superstitious will not pitch on Friday nights.
> The man who knows is not talking.

NONRESTRICTIVES:
> The taxes, which are reasonable, will be paid.
> Southpaws, who are superstitious, will not pitch on Friday nights.
> The man, who knows, is not talking.

The difference between restrictives and nonrestrictives is one of meaning, and the comma-pair signals that meaning. How many grandmothers do I have in the first sentence below (restrictive)? How many in the second (nonrestrictive)?

> My grandmother who smokes pot is ninety.
> My grandmother, who smokes pot, is ninety.

In the first sentence, I still have two grandmothers, since I am distinguishing one from the other by my restrictive phrase (no commas) as the one with the unconventional habit. In the second sentence, I have but one grandmother, about whom I am adding an interesting though nonessential, nonrestrictive detail within a pair of commas. Read the two aloud, and you will hear the difference in meaning, and how the pauses at the commas signal that difference. Commas are often optional, of course. The difference between a restrictive and a nonrestrictive meaning may sometimes be very slight. For example, you may take our recent bridegroom either way (but not halfway):

> That handsome man, in the ascot tie, is the groom. [nonrestrictive]
> That handsome man in the ascot tie is the groom. [restrictive]

Your meaning will dictate your choice. But use *pairs* of commas or none at all. Never separate subject and verb, or verb and object, with just one comma.

Some finer points. One comma of a pair enclosing an inserted remark may coincide with, and, in a sense, overlay, a comma "already there":

> In each box, a bottle was broken.
> In each box, however, a bottle was broken.
>
> The team lost, and the school was sick.
> The team lost, in spite of all, and the school was sick.
>
> The program will work, but the cost is high.
> The program will work, of course, but the cost is high.

Between the coordinate clauses, however, a semicolon might have been clearer:

> The team lost, in spite of all; and the school was sick.
> The program will work, of course; but the cost is high.

Beware: *however,* between commas, cannot substitute for *but,* as in the perfectly good sentence: "He wore a hat, *but* it looked terrible."

You would be using a comma where a full stop (period or semicolon) should be:

WRONG:
He wore a hat, however, it looked terrible.

RIGHT *(notice the two meanings):*
He wore a hat; however, it looked terrible.
He wore a hat, however; it looked terrible.

But a simple **, but** avoids both the ambiguity of the floating *however* and the ponderosity of anchoring it with a semicolon, fore or aft: "He wore a hat, but it looked terrible."

Another point. *But* may absorb the first comma of a pair enclosing an introductory remark (although it need not do so):

At any rate, he went.
But, at any rate, he went.
But at any rate, he went.
But [,] if we want another party, we had better clean up.
The party was a success, but [,] if we want another one, we had better clean up.

But avoid a comma *after* "but" in sentences like this:

I understand your argument, but [,] I feel your opponent has a stronger case.

Treat the "he said" and "she said" of dialogue as a regular parenthetical insertion, within commas, and without capitalizing, unless a new sentence begins:

"I'm going," he said, "whenever I get up enough nerve."
"I'm going," he said. "Whenever I get up enough nerve, I'm really going."

And American usage puts the comma *inside* ALL quotation marks:

"He is a nut," she said.
She called him a "nut," and walked away.

IV. THE LINKER. This is the usual one, linking on additional phrases and afterthoughts:

They went home, after too long a visit.
The book is too long, overloaded with examples.

It also links items in series. Again, the meaningful pause demands a comma:

> words, phrases, or clauses in a series
> to hunt, to fish, and to hike
> He went home, he went upstairs, and he could remember nothing.
> He liked oysters, soup, roast beef, and song.

Put a linker before the concluding *and*. By carefully separating all elements in a series, you keep alive a final distinction long ago lost in the daily press, the distinction Virginia Woolf makes (see p. 57): "urbane, polished, brilliant, imploring and commanding him . . . ." *Imploring and commanding* is syntactically equal to each one of the other modifiers in the series. If Woolf customarily omitted the last comma, as she does not, she could not have reached for that double apposition. The muscle would have been dead. These other examples of double apposition will give you an idea of its effectiveness:

> They cut out his idea, root and branch.
> He lost all his holdings, houses and lands.
> He loved to tramp the woods, to fish and hunt.

A comma makes a great deal of difference, of sense and distinction.

But adjectives in series, as distinct from nouns in series, change the game a bit. Notice the difference between the following two strings of adjectives:

> a good, unexpected, natural rhyme
> a good old battered hat

With adjectives in series, only your sense can guide you. If each seems to modify the noun directly, as in the first example above, use commas. If each seems to modify the total accumulation of adjectives and noun, as with *good* and *old* in the second phrase, do not use commas. Say your phrases aloud, and put your commas in the pauses that distinguish your meaning.

Finally, a special case. Dramatic intensity sometimes allows you to join clauses with commas instead of conjunctions:

> She sighed, she cried, she almost died.
> I couldn't do it, I tried, I let them all get away.
> It passed, it triumphed, it was a good bill.
> I came, I saw, I conquered.

The rhetorical intensity of this construction—the Greeks called it *asyndeton*—is obvious. The language is breathless, or grandly emphatic. As Aristotle once said, it is a person trying to say many things at once. The subjects repeat themselves, the verbs overlap, the idea accumulates a climax. By some psychological magic, the clauses of this construction usually come in three's. The comma is its sign. But unless you have a stylistic reason for such a flurry of clauses, go back to the normal comma and conjunction, the semicolon, or the period.

SEMICOLON AND COLON

Use the semicolon only where you could also use a period, unless desperate. This dogmatic formula, which I shall loosen up in a moment, has saved many a punctuator from both despair and a reckless fling of semicolons. Confusion comes from the belief that the semicolon is either a weak colon or a strong comma. It is most effective as neither. It is best, as we have seen (p. 47), in pulling together and contrasting two independent clauses that could stand alone as sentences:

> **The dress accents the feminine. The pants suit speaks for freedom.**
> **The dress accents the feminine; the pants suit speaks for freedom.**

This compression and contrast by semicolon can go even farther, allowing us to drop a repeated verb in the second element (note also how the comma marks the omission):

> **Golf demands the best of time and space; tennis demands the best of personal energy.**
> **Golf demands the best of time and space; tennis, the best of personal energy.**

Use a semicolon with a transitional word *(moreover, therefore, then, however, nevertheless)* to signal close contrast and connection:

> **He was lonely, blue, and solitary; moreover, his jaw ached.**

Used sparingly, the semicolon emphasizes your crucial contrasts; used recklessly, it merely clutters your page. *Never* use it as a colon: its effect is exactly opposite. A colon, as in the preceding sentence, signals the meaning to go ahead; a semicolon, as in this sentence, stops it. The colon is a green light; the semicolon is a stop sign.

Of course, you may occasionally need a semicolon to unscramble a long line of phrases and clauses, especially those in series and containing internal commas:

> **Composition is hard because we often must discover our ideas by writing them out, clarifying them on paper; because we must also**

find a clear and reasonable order for ideas the mind presents simultaneously; and because we must find, by trial and error, exactly the right words to convey our ideas and our feelings about them.

The colon waves the traffic on through the intersection: "Go right ahead," it says, "and you will find what you are looking for." The colon emphatically and precisely introduces a series, the clarifying detail, the illustrative example, and the formal quotation:

> The following players will start: Corelli, Smith, Jones, Baughman, and Stein.
> Pierpont lived for only one thing: money.
> In the end, it was useless: Adams really was too green.
> We remember Sherman's words: "War is hell."

PARENTHESIS AND DASH

The dash says aloud what the parenthesis whispers. Both enclose interruptions too extravagant for a pair of commas to hold. The dash is the more useful—since whispering tends to annoy—and will remain useful only if not overused. It can serve as a conversational colon. It can set off a concluding phrase—for emphasis. It can bring long introductory matters to focus, as in Freud's sentence on p. 55. It can insert a full sentence—a clause is really an incorporated sentence—directly next to a key word. The dash allows you to insert—with a kind of shout!—an occasional exclamation. You may even insert—and who would blame you?—an occasional question. The dash affords a structural complexity with all the tone and alacrity of talk.

With care, you can get much the same power from a parenthesis:

> Many philosophers have despaired (somewhat unphilosophically) of discovering any certainties whatsoever.
> Thus did Innocent III (I shall return to him shortly) inaugurate an age of horrors.
> But in such circumstances (see page 34), be cautious.
> Delay had doubled the costs (a stitch in time!), so the plans were shelved.

But dashes seem more generally useful, and here are some special points. When one of a pair of dashes falls where a comma would be, it absorbs the comma:

> If one wanted to go, he certainly could.
> If one wanted to go—whether invited or not—he certainly could.

Not so with the semicolon:

> He wanted to go — whether he was invited or not; she had more
> sense.

To indicate the dash, type two hyphens (--) flush against the words
they separate — not one hyphen between two spaces, nor a hyphen
spaced to look exactly like a hyphen.

Put commas and periods *outside* a parenthetical group of words
(like this one), even if the parenthetical group could stand alone as
a sentence (see the preceding "Innocent III" example). (But if you
make an actual full sentence parenthetical, put the period inside.)

BRACKETS

Brackets indicate your own words inserted or substituted within a
quotation from someone else: "Byron had already suggested that
[they] had killed John Keats." You have substituted "they" for "the
gentlemen of the *Quarterly Review*" to suit your own context; you
do the same when you interpolate a word of explanation: "Byron
had already suggested that the gentlemen of the *Quarterly Review*
[especially Croker] had killed John Keats." *Do not use parentheses:*
they mark the enclosed words as part of the original quotation. Don't
claim innocence because your typewriter lacks brackets. Just leave
spaces and draw them in later, or type slant lines and tip them with
pencil or with the underscore key:

$$[\cdot \cdot \cdot]$$

In the example below, you are pointing out with a *sic* (Latin for "so"
or "thus"), which you should not italicize, that you are reproducing
an error exactly as it appears in the text you are quoting:

> "On no occassion [sic] could we trust them."

Similarly you may give a correction after reproducing the error:

> "On the twenty-fourth [twenty-third], we broke camp."
> "In not one instance [actually, Baldwin reports several instances]
> did our men run under fire."

Use brackets when you need a parenthesis within a parenthesis:

> (see Donald Allenberg, *The Future of Television* [New York, 1973],
> pp. 15–16)

Your instructor will probably put brackets around the wordy parts of your sentences, indicating what you should cut:

In fact, [the reason] he liked it [was] because it was different.

QUOTATION MARKS AND ITALICS

Put quotation marks around quotations that "run directly into your text" (like this), but *not* around quotations set off from the text and indented. You normally inset poetry, as it stands, without quotation marks:

An aged man is but a paltry thing,
A tattered coat upon a stick, unless
Soul clap its hands and sing . . . .

But if you run it into your text, use quotation marks, with virgules (slants) showing the line-ends: "An aged man is but a paltry thing, / A tattered coat . . . ." Put periods and commas *inside* quotation marks; put semicolons and colons *outside:*

Now we understand the full meaning of "give me liberty, or give
   me death."
"This strange disease of modern life," in Arnold's words, remains
   uncured.
In Greece it was "know thyself"; in America it is "know thy
   neighbor."
He left after "Hail to the Chief": he could do nothing more.

Although logic often seems to demand the period or comma outside the quotation marks, convention has put them inside for the sake of appearance, even when the sentence ends in a single quoted word or letter:

Clara Bow was said to have "It."
Mark it with "T."

If you have seen the periods and commas outside, you were reading a British book or some of America's little magazines.

If you are quoting a phrase that already contains quotation marks, reduce the original double marks (") to single ones ('):

ORIGINAL	YOUR QUOTATION
Hamlet's "are you honest?" is easily explained.	He writes that "Hamlet's 'are you honest?' is easily explained."

Notice what happens when the quotation within your quotation falls at the end:

A majority of the informants thought *infer* **meant "imply."**	**Kirk reports that "a majority of the informants thought** *infer* **meant 'imply.' "**

And notice that a question mark or exclamation point falls between the single and the double quotation marks at the end of a quotation containing a quotation:

"Why do they call it 'the Hippocratic oath'?" she asked.
"Everything can't be 'cool'!" he said.

But heed the following exception:

"I heard someone say, 'Is anyone home?' " she declared.

Do not use *single* quotation marks for your own stylistic flourishes; use *double* quotation marks or, preferably, none:

It was indeed an "affair," but the passion was hardly "grand."
It was indeed an affair, but the passion was hardly grand.

Some "cool" pianists use the twelve-tone scale.

Once you have thus established this slang meaning of *cool,* you may repeat the word without quotation marks. In general, of course, you should favor that slang your style can absorb without quotation marks.

Do not use quotation marks for calling attention to words as words. Use italics (an underscore when typing) for the words, quotation marks for their meanings.

This is taking *tergiversation* **too literally.**
The word *struthious* **means "like an ostrich."**

Similarly, use italics for numbers as numbers and letters as letters:

He writes a *5* **like an** *s.*
Dot your *i*'s **and cross your** *t*'s.

But common sayings like "Watch your p's and q's" and "from A to Z" require no italics. Use quotation marks for titles *within* books and magazines: titles of chapters, articles, short stories, songs, and poems; use them also for titles of statues and paintings. But use italics for titles of books, newspapers, magazines, plays, movies, long poems, and for names of ships, trains, and airplanes. (See p. 159 for *The* in titles of newspapers and magazines.)

> Poe's description of how he wrote "The Raven" was attacked in the *Atlantic Monthly* [or: the *Atlantic*].
> We saw Michelangelo's "Pietà," a remarkable statue in white marble.
> We took the Santa Fe *Chief* from Chicago to Los Angeles.
> He read all of Frazer's *The Golden Bough*.
> His great-grandfather went down with the *Titanic*.
> She read it in the *New York Times*.

Italicize foreign words and phrases, unless they have been assimilated into English through usage (if your dictionary does not have a method for noting the distinction, consult one that has):

> The statement contained two clichés and one *non sequitur*.
> The author of this naïve exposé suffers from an *idée fixe*.

Use neither quotation marks nor italics for the Bible, for its books or parts (Genesis, Old Testament), for other sacred books (Koran, Talmud, Upanishad), or for famous documents like the Magna Carta, the Declaration of Independence, the Communist Manifesto, and the Gettysburg Address.

ELLIPSIS

1. Use three spaced periods . . . (the ellipsis mark) when you omit something within a quotation. Do *not* use them in your own text in place of a dash, or in mere insouciance.

2. If you omit the end of a sentence, add the period . . . ✔

3. If your omission falls after a completed sentence, add the three ellipsis marks to the period already there.✔. . .

I have put a check over the periods. Notice the difference in spacing. Note that each placement of the ellipsis means something different.

Here is an uncut passage, followed by a shortened version that shows in succession the three kinds of ellipsis, with the third appearing in two variations.

> To learn a language, learn as thoroughly as possible a few every-day sentences. This will educate your ear for all future pronunciations. It will give you a fundamental grasp of structure. Some of the details of grammar will begin to appear. It will give you confidence. If you go abroad, you can buy a newspaper and find your way back to the hotel.

(1)
To learn a language, learn . . . a few everyday sentences. This
(2)
will educate your ear . . . . It will give you a fundamental grasp
(3)   (3)
of structure. . . . It will give you confidence. . . . you can buy a
newspaper and find your way back to the hotel.

The three spaced dots of the ellipsis may fall on either side of other punctuation, to indicate exactly where you have omitted something within the text you are quoting:

In many instances . . . , our careful words are superfluous.
In many instances of human crisis, . . . words are superfluous.
In this sonnet, Shakespeare is well aware of the foolishness of
    self-pity: "And trouble deaf heaven with my bootless cries,/
    . . . and curse my fate, ..."

But you can omit the beginning and ending ellipses when you use a short quotation within a sentence:

Lincoln was determined that the Union, "cemented with the blood
of . . . the purest patriots," would not fail.

APOSTROPHE

Add apostrophe-*s* to form the singular possessive: *dog's life, hour's work, Marx's ideas.* Add apostrophe-*s* even to singular words already ending in *s: Yeats's poems, Charles's crown.* Plurals *not* ending in *s* also form the possessive by adding *'s: children's hour, women's rights.* But most plurals take the apostrophe after the *s* already there: *witches' sabbath, ten cents' worth, three days' time, the Joneses' possessions.*

I repeat, the rule for making singulars possessive is to add *'s* regardless of length and previous ending. (Some French names are exceptions: *Camus' works, Marivaux' life, Berlioz' Requiem.*) If your page grows too thick with double *s*'s, substitute a few pronouns for the proper names, or rephrase: *the death of Themistocles, the Dickens character Pip.* A caution: watch out for *its* and *it's, whose* and *who's, their* and *they're.*

The apostrophe can help to clarify clusters of nouns. These I have actually seen: *Alistair Jones Renown Combo, the church barbecue chicken sale, the uniform policeman training program, the members charter plane.* And of course, *teachers meeting* and *veterans insurance* are so common as to seem almost normal. But an apostrophe chips one more noun out of the block. It makes your meaning one word clearer, marking *teachers'* as a modifier, and distinguishing *teacher* from *teachers*. Inflections are helpful, and the written word needs all the help it can get: *Jones's Renowned, church's barbecued, uniformed policeman's, members' chartered*. Distinguish your modifiers, and keep your possessions.

Compound words take the *'s* on the last word only: *mother-in-law's hat, the brothers-in-law's attitude* (all the brothers-in-law have the same attitude), *somebody else's problem.* Joint ownerships may similarly take the *'s* only on the last word *(Bill and Mary's house),* but *Bill's and Mary's* house is more precise, and preferable.

Possessive pronouns have no apostrophe: *hers, its, theirs, yours, whose, oneself* (but *one's self,* if you are emphasizing the self). Note that *it's* means *it is,* and that *who's* means *who is;* for possession, use *its* and *whose.*

The double possessive uses both an *of* and an *'s: a friend of my mother's, a book of the teacher's, a son of the Joneses', an old hat of Mary's.* Note that the double possessive indicates one possession among several of the same kind: mother has several friends; the teacher, several books.

Use the apostrophe to indicate omissions: *the Spirit of '76, the Class of '02, can't, won't, don't.* Finally, use the apostrophe when adding a grammatical ending to a number, letter, sign, or abbreviation: *1920's;* his *3's* look like *8's; p's* and *q's;* he got four *A's;* too many *of's* and *and's;* she *X'd* each box; *K.O.'d* in the first round. (Some of these are also italic, or underlined when typed. See p. 151.)

HYPHEN

For clarity, hyphenate groups of words acting as one adjective or one adverb: *eighteenth-century attitude, early-blooming southern crocus, of-and-which disease.* Distinguish between a *high school,* and a *high-school teacher.* Similarly, hyphenate compound nouns when you need to distinguish, for example, *five sentence-exercises* from *five-sentence exercises.*

Hyphenate prefixes to proper names: *ex-Catholic, pro-Napoleon,* and all relatively new combinations like *anti-marriage.* Consult your dictionary.

Hyphenate after prefixes that demand emphasis or clarity: *ex-husband, re-collect* ("to collect again," as against *recollect,* "to remember"), *re-emphasize, pre-existent.*

When you must break a word at the end of a line, put your

hyphen where your dictionary marks the syllables with a dot: *syl·lables, syl-lables*. If you must break a hyphenated word, break it after the hyphen: *self-/sufficient*. Don't hyphenate an already hyphenated word: *self-suf-/ficient*. It's hard on the eyes and the printer. When you write for print, underline those line-end hyphens you mean to keep as hyphens, making a little equals sign: self=/sufficient.

Hyphenate suffixes to single capital letters (*T-shirt, I-beam, X-ray*). Hyphenate *ex-champions* and *self-reliances*. Hyphenate to avoid double *i*'s and triple consonants: *anti-intellectual, bell-like*. Hyphenate two-word numbers: *twenty-one, three-fourths*. Use the "suspensive" hyphen for hyphenated words in series: "We have ten-, twenty-five-, and fifty-pound sizes."

VIRGULE (SLANT, SLASH)

Spare this "little rod" (/), and don't spoil your work with the legalistic *and/or*. Don't write "bacon and/or eggs"; write "bacon or eggs, or both." Likewise, don't use it for a hyphen: not "male/female conflict" but "male-female conflict." Use the virgule when quoting poetry in your running text: "That time of year thou mayst in me behold / When yellow leaves, ..."

SPELLING

The dictionary is your best friend as you face the inevitable anxieties of spelling, but three underlying principles and some tricks of the trade can help immeasurably:

PRINCIPLE I. Letters represent sounds: proNUNciation can help you spell. No one proNOUNcing his words correctly would make the familiar errors of "similiar" and "enviorment." Simply sound out the letters: *envIRONment* and *goverNment* and *FebRUary* and *intRAmural*. Of course, you will need to be wary of some words *not* pronounced as spelled: *Wednesday*, pronounced "Wenzday," for instance. But sounding the letters can help your spellings. You can even say "convert*i*ble" and "indel*i*ble" and "plaus*i*ble" without sounding like a fool, and you can silently stress the *able* in words like "prob*able*" and "immov*able*" to remember the difficult distinction between words ending in *-ible*, and *-able*.

Consonants reliably represent their sounds. Remember that *c* and often *g* go soft before *i* and *e*. Consequently you must add a *k*

when extending words like *picnic* and *mimic — picnicKing, mimicKing*
— to keep them from rhyming with *slicing* or *dicing.* Conversely, you
just keep the *e* (where you would normally drop it) when making
peace into *peacEable* and *change* into *changEable,* to keep the *c* and *g*
soft.

Single *s* is pronounced *zh* in words like *vision, occasion, pleasure.*
Knowing that *ss* hushes ("sh-h-h") will keep you from errors like
occassion, which would sound like *passion.*

Vowels sound short and light before single consonants: *hat, pet,*
mit (*t*), *hop, mut* (*t*). When you add any vowel (including *y*) the first
vowel will say its name: *hate, Pete, mite, hoping, mutable.* Notice how
the *a* in *-able* keeps the main vowel saying its name in words like
unmistakable, likable, and *notable.* Therefore, to keep a vowel short,
protect it with a double consonant: *petting, hopping.* This explains
the troublesome *rr* in *occuRRence*: a single *r* would make it say *cure*
in the middle. *Putting* a golf ball and *putting* something on paper
must both use *tt* to keep from being pronounced *pewting.* Compare
stony with *sonny* and *bony* with *bonny.* The *y* is replacing the *e* in
stone and *bone,* and the rule is working perfectly. It works in any syllable that is accented: compare *forgeTTable* as against *markeTing,*
begiNNing as against *buttoNing,* and *compeLLing* as against *traveLing.*

Likewise, when *full* combines and loses its stress, it also loses
an *l*. Note the single and double *l* in *fulFILLment.* Similarly, *SOUL-*
ful, GRATEful, AWful — even *SPOONful.*

PRINCIPLE II. This is the old rule of *i* before *e,* and its famous
exceptions.

> *I* **before** *e*
> **Except after** *c,*
> **Or when sounded like** *a*
> **As in** neighbor **and** *weigh.*

It works like a charm (*achieve, believe; receive, conceive*). Note that *c*
needs an *e* to make it sound like *s*. Remember also that *leisure* was
once pronounced "lay-sure," and *foreign,* "forayn," and *heifer,*
"hayfer." Memorize these important exceptions: *seize, weird, either,*
sheik, forfeit, counterfeit, protein. Note that all are pronounced "ee"
(with a little crowding) and that the *e* comes first. Then note that
another small group goes the opposite way, having a long *i* sound as
in German "Heil": *height, sleight, seismograph, kaleidoscope. Financier,*
another exception, follows its French origin and its original sound.
Deity sounds both vowels as spelled.

PRINCIPLE III. Most big words, following the Latin or French from which they came, spell their sounds letter for letter. Look up the derivations of the words you misspell (note that double *s,* and explain it). You will never again have trouble with *desperate* and *separate* once you discover that the first comes from *de-spero,* "without hope," and that SePARate divides equals, the PAR values in stocks or golf. Nor with *definite* or *definitive,* once you see the kinship of both with *finite* and *finish.* Derivations can also help you a little with the devilment of *-able* and *-ible,* since, except for a few ringers, the *i* remains from Latin, and the *-ables* are either French (*ami-able*) or Anglo-Saxon copies (*workable*). Knowing origins can help at crucial points: *resemblAnce* comes from Latin *simulAre,* "to copy"; *existEnce* comes from Latin *existEre;* "to stand forth."

The biggest help comes from learning the common Latin prefixes, which, by a process of assimilation (*ad-similis,* "like to like"), account for the double consonants at the first syLLabic joint of so many of our words:

AD- **(toward, to):** *abbreviate* **(shorten down),** *accept* **(grasp to).**
CON- **(with):** *collapse* **(fall with),** *commit* **(send with).**
DIS- **(apart):** *dissect* **(cut apart),** *dissolve* **(loosen apart).**
IN- **(into):** *illuminate* **(shine into),** *illusion* **(playing into).**
IN- **(not):** *illegal* **(not lawful),** *immature* **(not ripe).**
INTER- **(between):** *interrupt* **(break between),** *interrogate* **(ask between).**
OB- **(toward, to):** *occupy* **(take in),** *oppose* **(put to),** *offer* **(carry to).**
SUB- **(under):** *suffer* **(bear under),** *suppose* **(put down).**
SYN- **("together"—this one is Greek):** *symmetry* **(measuring together),** *syllogism* **(logic together).**

Spelling takes a will, an eye, and an ear. And a dictionary. Keep a list of your favorite enemies. Memorize one or two a day. Write them in the air in longhand. Visualize them. Imagine a blinking neon sign, with the wicked letters red and tall—d e f i n I t e—d e f i n I t e. Then print them once, write them twice, and blink them a few times more as you go to sleep. But best of all, make up whatever devices you can—the crazier the better—to remember the tricky parts:

DANCE attenDANCE.
EXISTENCE is TENSE.
There's IRON in this enviRONment.
The resisTANCE took its STANCE.
There's an ANT on the defendANT.
LOOSE as a goose.

LOSE loses an o.
ALLOT isn't A LOT.
Already isn't ALL RIGHT.
I for gaIety.
The LL in paraLLel gives me *el.*
PURr in PURsuit.

When an unaccented syllable leads to misspelling, you can also get some help by trying to remember a version of the word that accents the troublesome syllable: acad*e*my — acaDEMIC; defin*i*tely — defiNITION; irrit*a*ble — irriTATE; prep*a*ration — prePARE.

Many foreign words, though established in English, retain their native diacritical marks, which aid in pronunciation: *naïveté, résumé, séance, tête-à-tête, façade, Fräulein, mañana, vicuña.* Many names are similarly treated: *Müller, Gödel, Göttingen, Poincaré, Brontë, Noël Coward, García Lorca, Havlíček.* As always, your dictionary is your best guide, as it is, indeed, to all words transliterated to English from different alphabets and systems of writing (Russian, Arabic, Chinese, Japanese, and so on).

Here are more of the perpetual headaches:

accept — except	exaggerate
accommodate	explain — explanation
acknowledgment — judgment	familiar — similar
advice — advise	forward — foreword
affect — effect	genius — ingenious* — ingenuous*
all right* — a lot*	height — eighth
allusion — illusion — disillusion*	hypocrisy — democracy
analysis — analyzing	irritable
argue — argument	its — it's*
arrangement	lonely — loneliness
businessman	marriage — marital — martial
capital — capitol*	misspell — misspelling
censor — censure	Negroes — heroes — tomatoes
committee	obstacle
complement — compliment	possession
continual — continuous*	primitive
controversy	principal — principle*
council — counsel — consul*	proceed — precede — procedure
criticize — criticism	rhythm
curriculum* — career —	questionnaire
occurrence	stationary — stationery
decide — divide — devices	succeed — successful
desert — dessert	suppressed
dilemma — condemn	their — they're
disastrous	truly
discreet — discrete*	until — till
embarrassment — harassment	unnoticed
eminent — imminent —	weather — whether
immanent	who's — whose*

* In the Glossary of Usage.

CAPITALIZATION

You know about sentences and names, certainly; but the following points are troublesome. Capitalize:

1. Names of races, languages, and religions—Negro, Caucasian, Mongolian, Protestant, Jewish, Christian, Roman Catholic, Indian, French, English. But "blacks and whites in this neighborhood," "black entrepreneurs," "white storekeepers"—especially in phrases that contrast blacks and whites, since *white* is never capitalized.

2. North, south, east, and west *only when they are regions*—the mysterious East, the new Southwest—or parts of proper nouns: the West Side, East Lansing.

3. The *complete* names of churches, rivers, hotels, and the like—the First Baptist Church, the Mark Hopkins Hotel, the Suwannee River (not First Baptist church, Mark Hopkins hotel, Suwannee river).

4. All words in titles, except prepositions, articles, and conjunctions. But capitalize even these if they come first or last, or if they are longer than four letters—"I'm Through with Love," *Gone with the Wind,* "I'll Stand By," *In Darkest Africa.* Capitalize nouns, adjectives, and prefixes in hyphenated compounds—*The Eighteenth-Century Background, The Anti-Idealist* (but *The Antislavery Movement*). But hyphenated single words, the names of numbered streets, and the written-out numbers on your checks are *not* capitalized after the hyphen: *Self-fulfillment, Re-examination. Forty-second Street, Fifty-four . . . Dollars.*

When referring to magazines and newspapers in sentences and footnotes, drop the *The* as part of the title: the *Atlantic Monthly,* the *Kansas City Star.* (Euphony and sense preserve *The* for a few: *The New Yorker, The Spectator.*) But in lists and bibliographies, retain *The* if a part of the full title.

5. References to a specific section of a work—the Index, his Preface, Chapter 1, Volume IV, Act II, but "scene iii" is usually not capitalized because its numerals are also in lower case.

6. Abstract nouns, when you want emphasis, serious or humorous—". . . the truths contradict, so what is Truth?"; Very Important Person; the Ideal.

Do not capitalize the seasons—spring, winter, midsummer.

Do not capitalize after a colon, unless what follows is normally capitalized:

> **Again we may say with Churchill: "Never have so many owed so much to so few."**
> *Culture, People, Nature: An Introduction to General Anthropology* **[title of book]**
> **Many lost everything in the earthquake: their homes had vanished along with their supplies, their crops, their livestock.**

Do not capitalize proper nouns serving as common nouns: *china, cognac, napoleon* (a pastry), *chauvinist, watt* (electricity). (Usage divides on some proper adjectives: *French [french] pastry, Cheddar [cheddar] cheese, German [german] measles, Venetian [venetian] blinds.* Breeds of animals, as in *Welsh terrier,* and products of a definite origin, as in *Scotch whiskey,* are less uncertain.) When in doubt, your best guide, as in spelling, is your dictionary.

EXERCISES

1 Punctuate the following sentences. Add italics where needed. Which sentences might work well as two sentences, assuming no change in the wording? Which arrangement would you prefer?

1. Like the farmer in Frost's Mending Wall, some people believe that Good fences make good neighbors.

2. We find however that the greatest expense in renovation will be for labor not for materials.

3. C. Wright Mills The Power Elite which even after twenty years is still one of the finest examples of sociological analysis available ought to be required reading in any elementary sociology course. (Make Mills possessive.)

4. Here see means understand and audience stands for all the books readers.

5. They took chemistry fine arts history and English.

6. We met June 1 1978 to discuss the problem which continued to plague us.

7. For him the most important letter between A and Z is I.

8. A faithful sincere friend he remained loyal to his roommate even after the unexpected turn of events.

9. Why does the raven keep crying Nevermore! he asked.

10. Stephano and Trinculo are the comics of the play never presented as complete characters they are not taken seriously.

11. Readers of Joseph Heller's book Catch-22 a comic novel about World War II seem to react in one of two ways either they love the

book or they can't stand it in either case the book seems to arouse their passions.

12. In America said the Chinese lecturer people sing Home Sweet Home in China they stay there.

13. Depressed refusing to face the reality of his situation he killed himself it was as simple as that.

14. The boys favorite books were Huckleberry Finn the Bible especially Ecclesiastes and Henry David Thoreaus Walden.

15. The book deals with the folly of war its stupidity its cruelty however in doing this the author brings in too many characters repeats episodes over and over and spoils his comedy by pressing too hard.

16. To let him go unpunished was unthinkable to punish him unbearable.

17. Though she was a junior college instructor teaching advanced calculus given at night during the winter did not intimidate her. (Use dashes.)

18. Walter he was confused at the time asked what time does the Reds game start this afternoon? (Add parentheses and capitals.)

19. Some groovy singers seem stuck in one groove.

20. Germaine Greer's The Female Eunuch is a book to be remembered especially for phrases like I'm sick of peering at the world through false eyelashes and I'm a woman not a castrate.

2 Make a list of your ten most frequent misspellings. Then keep it handy and active, removing your conquests and adding your new troubles.

3 Capitalize the following, where necessary:

go west, young man.
the south left the union.
the introduction to *re-establishing toryism.*
the tall black spoke french.
she loved the spring.
health within seconds (book)
clear through life in time (book)
a doberman pinscher
the methodist episcopal church

the missouri river
my christian name begins with *c.*
the new york public library
the neo-positivistic approach (book)
the st. louis post-dispatch (add italics)
twenty-five dollars (on a check)
33 thirty-third street
rubber was first vulcanized in the mid-nineteenth century.

Handbook C
A Glossary of Usage

Speech keeps a daily pressure on writing, and writing returns the compliment, exacting sense from new twists in the spoken language and keeping old senses straight. Usage, generally, is "the way they say it." Usage is the current in the living stream of language; it keeps us afloat, it keeps us fresh—as it sweeps us along. But to distinguish yourself as a writer, you must always battle it, must always swim upstream. You may say, "Hooja-eatwith?"; but you will write: "With whom did they compare themselves? With the best, with whoever seemed admirable." Usage is, primarily, talk; and talk year by year gives words differing social approval, and differing meanings. Words move from the gutter to the penthouse, and back down the elevator shaft. *Bull,* a four-letter Anglo-Saxon word, was unmentionable in Victorian circles. One had to use *he-cow,* if at all. Phrases and syntactical patterns also have their fashions, mostly bad. *Like me* changes to *like I do; this type of thing* becomes *this type thing; -wise,* after centuries of dormancy in only a few words (*likewise, clockwise, otherwise*), suddenly sprouts out the end of everything: *budgetwise, personalitywise, beautywise, prestigewise.* Suddenly, everyone is saying *hopefully.* As usual, the marketplace changes more than your money.

But the written language has always refined the language of the marketplace. The Attic Greek of Plato and Aristotle (as Aristotle's remarks about local usages show) was distilled from commercial exchange. Cicero and Catullus and Horace polished their currency against the archaic and the Greek. Mallarmé claimed that Poe had given *un sens plus pur aux mots de la tribu* — which Eliot rephrases for himself: "to purify the dialect of the tribe." It is the very nature of writing so to do; it is the writer's illusion that he has done so:

> I have laboured to refine our language to grammatical purity, and to clear it from colloquial barbarisms, licentious idioms, and irregular combinations. Something, perhaps, I have added to the elegance of its construction, and something to the harmony of its cadence.

— wrote Samuel Johnson in 1752 as he closed his *Rambler* papers. And he had almost done what he hoped. He was to shape English writing for the next hundred and fifty years, until it was ready for another dip in the stream and another purification. His work, moreover, lasts. We would not imitate it now; but we can read it with pleasure, and imitate its enduring drive for excellence.

Johnson goes on to say in the preface to his great *Dictionary* that he has "rarely admitted any word not authorized by former writers." Writers provide the second level of usage, the paper money. But even this usage requires principle. If we accept "what the best writers use," we still cannot tell whether it is sound: we may be aping their bad habits. Usage is only a court of first appeal, where we can say little more than "He said it." Beyond that helpless litigation, we can test our writing by reason, and by simple principles: clarity is good, economy is good, ease is good, gracefulness is good, fullness is good, forcefulness is good. As with all predicaments on earth, we judge by appeal to principles, and we often find principles in conflict. Is it economical but unclear? Is it full but cumbersome? Is it clear but too colloquial for grace? Careful judgment will give the ruling.

THE GLOSSARY

a, an. *A* goes before consonants and *an* before vowels. But use *a* before *h* sounded in a first syllable: *a hospital, a hamburger.* Use *an* before a silent h: *an honor, an heir, an hour.* Use *a* before vowels pronounced as consonants: *a use, a euphemism.*

Abbreviations. Use only those conventional abbreviations your reader can easily recognize: *Dr., Mr., Mrs., Ms., Messrs.* (for two or more men, pronounced "messers," as in *Messrs. Adams, Pruitt, and Williams*), *Jr., St., Esq.* (Esquire, following a British gentleman's name, between commas and with *Mr.* omitted), *S.J.* (Society of Jesus, also following a name). All take periods. College degrees are equally recognizable: *A.B., M.A., Ph.D., D. Litt., M.D., LL.D.* Similarly, dates and times: B.C., A.D., A.M., P.M. Though these are conventionally printed as small capitals, regular capitals in your classroom papers are perfectly acceptable as are "lowercase" letters for a.m. and p.m. Write them without commas: *2000 B.C. was Smith's estimate.* A number of familiar abbreviations go without periods: *TV, FBI, USSR, USA, YMCA,* though periods are perfectly OK or O.K. Certain scientific phrases also go without periods, especially when combined with figures: *55 mph, 300 rpm, 4000 kwh.* But *U.N.* and *U.S. delegation* are customary. Note that *U.S.* serves only as an adjective; write out *the United States,* serving as a noun.

Abbreviations conventional in running prose, unitalicized, are "e.g." (*exempli gratia,* "for example"), "i.e." (*id est,* "that is"), "etc." (*et cetera,* better written out "and so forth") and "viz." (*videlicet,* pronounced "vi-DEL-uh-sit," meaning "that is," "namely"). These are followed by either commas or colons after the period:

The commission discovered three frequent errors in management, i.e., failure to take appropriate inventories, erroneous accounting, and inattention to costs.
The semester included some outstanding extracurricular programs, e.g.: a series of lectures on civil rights, three concerts, and a superb performance of *Oedipus Rex.*

The abbreviation *vs.,* usually italicized, is best spelled out, unitalicized, in your text: "The antagonism of Capulet versus Montague runs throughout the play." The abbreviation *c.* or *ca.,* standing for *circa* ("around") and used with approximate dates in parentheses, is italicized: "Higden wrote *Polychronicon* (*c.* 1350)." For further abbreviations in footnoting, see Chapter 9, "The Research Paper," pp. 99–101.

Above. For naturalness and effectiveness, avoid such references as "The above statistics are . . . . ," and "The above speaks for itself." Simply use "These" or "This."

Adapt, adopt. To *adapt* is to modify something to fit a new purpose. To *adopt* is to take it over as it is.

Advice, advise. Frequently confused. *Advice* is what you get when advisers *advise* you.

Affect, effect. *Affect* means "to produce an *effect.*" Avoid *affect* as a noun; just say *feeling* or *emotion. Affective* is a technical term for *emotional* or *emotive,* which are clearer.

Aggravate. Means to add gravity to something already bad enough. Avoid using it to mean "irritate."

WRONG	RIGHT
He aggravated his mother.	The rum aggravated his mother's fever.

All, all of. Use *all* without the *of* wherever you can to economize: *all this, all that, all those, all the people, all her lunch.* But some constructions need *of: all of them, all of Faulkner.*

All ready, already. Two different meanings. *All ready* means that everything is ready; *already* means "by this time."

All right, alright. *Alright* is not *all right;* you are confusing it with the spelling of *already.*

Allusion, illusion, disillusion. The first two are frequently confused, and *disillusion* is frequently misspelled *disallusion.* An *allusion* is a reference to something; an illusion is a mistaken conception. You disillusion someone by bringing him back to hard reality from his illusions.

Alot. You mean *a lot,* not *allot.*

Ambiguous. If your instructor marks *Amb* in the margin, he means "this has two meanings," one of which you probably have not noticed. Have you said, "Socrates admitted he was wrong"? This could mean that Socrates admitted that he, Socrates, was wrong, or it could mean that Socrates admitted that Crito was wrong. Check your statements to see that they cannot mean something else to the innocent reader.

Among. See *Between.*

Amount of, number of. Use *amount* with general heaps of things; use number with amounts that might be counted: *a small amount of interest, a large number of votes.*

And/or. An ungainly thought stopper. See p. 155.

Anxious. Use to indicate *Angst,* agony, and anxiety. Does not mean cheerful expectation: "He was *anxious* to get started." Use *eager* instead.

Any. Do not overuse as a modifier:

POOR	GOOD
She was the best of any senior in the class.	She was the best senior in the class.
If any people know the answer, they aren't talking.	If anyone knows the answer, he's not talking.

Add *other* when comparing likes: "She was better than *any other* senior in the class." But "This junior was better than any senior."

Any more. Written as two words, except when an adverb in negatives and questions:

She never wins *anymore.*
Does she play *anymore?*

Anyplace, someplace. Use *anywhere* and *somewhere* (adverbs), unless you mean "any *place*" and "some *place*."

Appear. Badly overworked for *seem.*

Appreciate. Means "recognize the worth of." Do not use to mean simply "understand."

LOOSE	CAREFUL
I appreciate your position.	I understand your position.
I appreciate that your position is grotesque.	I realize that your position is grotesque.

Area. Drop it. *In the area of finance* means *in finance,* and *conclusive in all areas* means simply *conclusive,* or *conclusive in all departments (subjects, topics).* Be specific.

Around. Do not use for *about:* it will seem to mean "surrounding."

POOR	GOOD
Around thirty people came.	About thirty people came.
He sang at around ten o'clock.	He sang at about ten o'clock.

As. Use where the cigarette people have *like:* "It tastes good, *as* a goody should," or "it taste good the way a goody should." (See also *Like.*)

Do not use for *such as:* "Many things, *as* nails, hats, toothpicks. . . ." Write "Many things, *such as* nails . . . ."

Do not use *as* for *because* or *since;* it is ambiguous:

AMBIGUOUS	PRECISE
As I was walking, I had time to think.	Because I was walking, I had time to think.

As if. Takes the subjunctive: ". . . as if he *were* cold."

As of, as of now. Avoid, except for humor. Use *at*, or *now*, or delete entirely.

POOR	IMPROVED
He left as of ten o'clock.	He left at ten o'clock.
As of now, I've sworn off.	I've just sworn off.

As to. Use only at the beginning of a sentence: "As to his first allegation, I can only say . . . ." Change it to *about*, or omit it, within a sentence: "He knows nothing *about* the details"; "He is not sure [as to] [whether] they are right."

As well as. You may mean only *and*. Check it out. Avoid such ambiguities as *The Commons voted as well as the Lords.*

Aspect. Overused. Try *side, part, portion.* See *Jargon.*

At. Do not use after *where*. "Where is it at?" means "Where is it?"

Awhile, a while. You usually want the adverb: *linger awhile, the custom endured awhile longer.* If you want the noun, emphasizing a period of time, make it clear: *the custom lasted for a while.*

Bad, badly. See *Good, well* and p. 132.

Balance, bulk. Make them mean business, as in "He deposited the balance of his allowance" and "The bulk of the crop was ruined." Do not use them for people.

POOR	IMPROVED
The balance of the class went home.	The rest of the class went home.
The bulk of the crowd was indifferent.	Most of the crowd was indifferent.

Basis. Drop it: *on a daily basis* means *daily.*

Be sure and. Write *be sure to.*

Because of, due to. See *Due to.*

Besides. Means "in addition to," not "other than."

POOR	IMPROVED
Something besides smog was the cause [unless smog was also a cause].	Something other than smog was the cause.

Better than. Unless you really mean *better than,* use *more than.*

POOR	IMPROVED
The lake was better than two miles across.	The lake was more than two miles across.

Between, among. *Between* ("by twain") has *two* in mind; *among* has more than two. *Between,* a preposition, takes an object; *between us, between you and me.* ("Between you and I" is sheer embarrassment; see *me,* below.) *Between* also indicates geographical placing: "It is midway between Chicago, Detroit, and Toledo." "The grenade fell between Jones and me and the gatepost"; but "The grenade fell among the fruit stands." "Between every building was a plot of petunias" conveys the idea, however nonsensical "between a building" is. "Between all the buildings were plots of petunias" would be better, though still a compromise.

Bimonthly, biweekly. Careless usage has damaged these almost beyond recognition, confusing them with *semimonthly* and *semiweekly.* For clarity, better say "every two months" and "every two weeks."

But, cannot but. "He can but fail" is old but usable. After a negative, however, the natural turn in *but* causes confusion:

POOR	IMPROVED
He cannot but fail	He can only fail.
He could not doubt but that it	He could not doubt that it . . . .
He could not help but take	He could not help taking . . . .

When *but* means "except," it is a preposition. "Everybody laughed but me."

But that, but what. Colloquial redundancies.

POOR	IMPROVED
There is no doubt but that John's is the best steer.	There is no doubt that John's is the best steer.
	John's is clearly the best steer.
There is no one but what would enjoy it.	Anyone would enjoy it.

Can, may (could, might). *Can* means ability; *may* asks permission, and expresses possibility. *Can I go?* means, strictly, "Have I the physical capability to go?" In speech, *can* usually serves for both ability and permission, though the salesgirl will probably say, properly, "May I help you?" In assertions, the distinction is clear: "He can do it." "He may do it." "If he can, he may." Keep these distinctions clear in your writing.

Could and might are the past tenses, but when used in the present time they are subjunctive, with shades of possibility, and hence politeness: "Could you come next Tuesday?" "Might I inquire about your plans?" Could may mean ability almost as strongly as can: "I'm sure he could do it." But could and might are usually subjunctives, expressing doubt:

Perhaps he could make it, if he tries.
I might be able to go, but I doubt it.

Cannot, can not. Use either, depending on the rhythm and emphasis you want. Can not emphasizes the not slightly.

Can't hardly, couldn't hardly. Use can hardly, could hardly, since hardly carries the negative sense.

Can't help but. A marginal mixture in speech of two clearer and more formal ideas I can but regret and I can't help regretting. Avoid it in writing.

Capital, capitol. Frequently confused. You mean capital, the head thing (from Latin capitalis, "of the head") whether writing of the head city of a state, provincial (Canada), or national government, the head letter of a sentence, or the top (the "head") of a Greek column. Capitol, capitalized, is the special name of the Temple of Jupiter on the Capitoline Hill in Rome, and also of the Capitol building, where Congress sits in Washington, D.C., or the Capitol Hill in Washington, on which the Capitol stands (the American founders named their new headquarters, and the hill they stood on, after the Roman ones). Confusion comes especially when you think of Washington, which is the capital, not the capitol, of the United States. When not capitalized, a capitol is the building where a state legislature sits.

Case. Chop out this deadwood:

POOR	IMPROVED
In many cases, ants survive. . . .	Ants often . . . .
In such a case, surgery is recommended.	Then surgery is recommended.
In case he goes	If he goes . . . .
Everyone enjoyed himself, except in a few scattered cases.	Almost everyone enjoyed himself.

Cause, result. Since *all* events are both causes and results, suspect yourself of wordiness if you write either word.

WORDY	ECONOMICAL
The invasions caused depopulation of the country.	The invasion depopulated the country.
He lost as a result of poor campaigning.	He lost because his campaign was poor.

Cause-and-effect relationship. Verbal adhesive tape. Recast the sentence, with some verb other than the wordy *cause:*

POOR	IMPROVED
Othello's jealousy rises in a cause-and-effect relationship when he sees the handkerchief.	Seeing the handkerchief arouses Othello's jealousy.

Censor, censure. Frequently confused. A *censor* cuts out objectionable passages. *To censor* is to cut or prohibit. *To censure* is to condemn: "The *censor censored* some parts of the play, and *censured* the author as an irresponsible drunkard."

Center around. A physical impossibility. Make it *centers on,* or *revolves around,* or *concerns,* or *is about.*

Clichés. Don't use unwittingly. But they can be effective. There are two kinds: (1) the rhetorical—*tried and true, the not too distant future, sadder but wiser, in the style to which she had become accustomed;* (2) the proverbial—*apple of his eye, skin of your teeth, sharp as a tack, quick as a flash, twinkling of an eye.* The rhetorical ones are clinched by sound alone; the proverbial are metaphors caught in the popular fancy. Proverbial clichés can lighten a dull passage. You may even revitalize them, since they are frequently dead metaphors (see pp. 76–77). Avoid the rhetorical clichés unless you turn them to your advantage: *tried and untrue, gladder and wiser, a future not too distant.*

Complement, compliment. Frequently confused. *Complement* is a completion; *compliment* is a flattery: "When the regiment reached its full *complement* of recruits, the general gave it a flowery *compliment.*"

Concept. Often jargonish and wordy.

POOR	IMPROVED
The concept of multiprogramming allows	Multiprogramming allows . . . .

Contact. Don't *contact* anyone: call him, write him, find him, tell him.

Continual, continuous. You can improve your writing by *continual* practice, but the effort cannot be *continuous*. The first means "frequently repeated"; the second, "without interruption."

It requires *continual* practice.
There was a *continuous* line of clouds.

Contractions. We use them constantly in conversation: *don't, won't, can't, shouldn't, isn't.* Avoid them in writing, or your prose will seem too chummy. But use one now and then when you want some colloquial emphasis: *You can't go home again.*

Could, might. See *Can, may.*

Could care less. You mean *couldn't care less.* Speech has worn off the *n't,* making the words say the opposite of what you mean. A person who cares a great deal could care a great deal less; one who does not care *"couldn't* care less": he's already at rock bottom.

Could of, would of. Phonetic misspellings of *could've* ("could have"), and *would've* ("would have"). In writing, spell them all the way out: *could have* and *would have*.

Couldn't hardly. Use *could hardly.*

Council, counsel, consul. *Council* is probably the noun you mean: a group of deliberators. *Counsel* is usually the verb "to advise." But *counsel* is also a noun: an adviser, an attorney, and their advice. Check your dictionary to see that you are writing what you mean. A *counselor* gives you his *counsel* about your courses, which may be submitted to an academic *council.* A *consul* is an official representing your government in a foreign country.

Curriculum. The plural is *curricula,* though *curriculums* will get by in informal prose. The adjective is *curricular.*

Definitely. A high-school favorite, badly overused.

Discreet, discrete. Frequently confused. *Discreet* means someone tactful and judicious; *discrete* means something separate and distinct: "He was *discreet* in examining each *discrete* part of the evidence."

Disinterested. Does not mean "uninterested" nor "indifferent." *Disinterested* means impartial, without private interests in the issue.

WRONG	RIGHT
You seem disinterested in the case.	You seem uninterested in the case.
	The judge was disinterested and perfectly fair.
He was disinterested in it.	He was indifferent to it.

Double negative. A negation that cancels another negation, making it accidentally positive: "He couldn't hardly" indicates that "He could easily," the opposite of its intended meaning. "They can't win nothing" really says that they *must* win something.

But some doubled negations carry an indirect emphasis — a mild irony, really — in such tentative assertions as "One cannot be certain that she will not prove to be the century's greatest poet," or "a not unattractive offer."

Due to. Never begin a sentence with "*Due* to circumstances beyond his control, he . . . ." *Due* is an adjective and must always relate to a noun or pronoun: "The catastrophe *due to* circumstances beyond his control was unavoidable," or "The catastrophe was *due* to circumstances beyond his control" (predicate adjective). But you are still better off with *because of, through, by,* or *owing to. Due to* is usually a symptom of wordiness, especially when it leads to *due to the fact that,* a venerable piece of plumbing meaning *because.*

WRONG	RIGHT
He resigned *due to* sickness.	He resigned *because of* sickness.
He succeeded *due to* hard work.	He succeeded *through* hard work.
He lost his shirt *due to* leaving it in the locker room.	He lost his shirt *by* leaving it in the locker room.
The Far East will continue to worry the West, *due to* a general social upheaval.	The Far East will continue to worry the West, *owing to* a general social upheaval.
The program failed *due to the fact that* a recession had set in.	The program failed *because* a recession had set in.

Either, neither. One of two, taking a singular verb: *Either is a good candidate, but neither speaks well. Either . . . or (neither . . . nor)* are paralleling conjunctions. See pp. 53–54.

Eminent, imminent, immanent. Often confused. *Eminent* is something that stands out; *imminent* is something about to happen. *Immanent,* much less common, is a philosophical term for something spiritual "remaining within, indwelling." You usually mean *eminent*.

Enormity. Means "atrociousness"; does not mean "enormousness."

the *enormity* of the crime
the *enormousness* of the mountain

Enthuse. Don't use it; it coos and gushes:

WRONG	RIGHT
She *enthused* over her new dress.	She gushed on and on about her new dress.
He was *enthused*.	He was *enthusiastic*.

Environment. Frequently misspelled *enviorment* or *envirnment*. It is business jargon, unless you mean the world around us.

WORDY	IMPROVED
in an MVT environment	in MVT; with MVT; under MVT
He works in the environment of cost analysis.	He analyzes costs.

Equally as good. A redundant mixture of two choices, *as good as* and *equally good.* Use only one of these at a time.

Everyday, every day. You wear your *everyday* clothes *every day*.

Everyone, everybody. Avoid the common mismatching *their*:

"Everyone does *his* [or *her* but not *their*] own thing."

Exists. Another symptom of wordiness.

POOR	IMPROVED
a system like that which exists at the university	a system like that at the university

The fact that. Deadly with *due to*, and usually wordy by itself.

POOR	IMPROVED
The fact that Rome fell *due to* moral decay is clear.	*That* Rome fell *through* moral decay is clear.
This disparity is in part *a result of the fact that* some of the best indicators make their best showings in an expanding market.	This disparity arises in part *because* some of the best indicators ....
In view of the fact that more core core is installed	*Because* more core ....

Factor. Avoid it. We've used it to death. Try *element* when you mean "element." Look for an accurate verb when you mean "cause."

POOR	IMPROVED
The increase in female employment is a factor in juvenile delinquency.	The increase in female employment has contributed to juvenile delinquency.
Puritan self-sufficiency was an important factor in the rise of capitalism.	Puritan self-sufficiency favored the rise of capitalism.

Farther, further. The first means distance; the second means time or figurative distance. You look *farther* and consider *further*.

Feasible. See *Viable*.

Fewer, less. See *Less, few*.

The field of. Try to omit it — you usually can — or bring the metaphor to life. It is trite and wordy.

POOR	IMPROVED
He is studying in the field of geology.	He is studying geology.

Firstly. Archaic. Trim all such terms to *first, second, third,* and so on.

Flaunt, flout. *Flaunt* means to parade, to wave impudently; *flout* means to scoff at. The first is metaphorical; the second, not: "She *flaunted* her wickedness and *flouted* the police."

For. See p. 142.

Former, latter. Passable, but they often make the reader look back. Repeating the antecedents is clearer.

POOR	IMPROVED
The Athenians and Spartans were always in conflict. *The former* had a better civilization; *the latter* had a better army.	The Athenians and Spartans were always in conflict. Athens had the better culture; Sparta, the better army.

Further. See *Farther*.

Good, well. *Good* is the adjective: *good time*. *Well* is the adverb: *well done*. In verbs of feeling, we are caught in the ambiguities of health. *I feel good* is more accurate than *I feel well*, because *well* may mean that your feelers are in working order. But *I feel well* is also an honest statement: "I feel that I am well." Ask yourself what your readers might misunderstand from your statements, and you will use these two confused terms clearly.

Got, gotten. Both acceptable. Your rhythm and emphasis will decide. America prefers the older *gotten* in many phrases; Britain goes mainly for *got*.

Hanged, hung. *Hanged* is the past of *hang* only for the death penalty.

They hung the rope and hanged the man.

Hardly. Watch the negative here. "I can't *hardly*" means "I *can* easily." Write: "One can hardly conceive the vastness."

His/her, his (her). Shift to the neutral plural, or otherwise rephrase to avoid this awkwardness. *His* stands for both sexes, if you can stand it.

Historically. A favorite windy throat-clearer. Badly overused.

History. The *narrative*, written or oral, of events, not the events themselves. Therefore, avoid the redundancy *"recorded* history," likewise *"annals* of history," *"chronicles* of history." *History* alone will suffice: "Archaeologists have uncovered evidence of events previously unknown to history"; "World War II was the most devastating conflict in history."

Hopefully. An inaccurate dangler, a cliché. "Hopefully, they are at work" does not mean that they are working hopefully. Simply use "I hope" or "one hopes" (but *not* "it is hoped"): not "They are a symbol of idealism, and, hopefully, are representative," but "They are a symbol of idealism and are, one hopes, representative."

However. Initial *however* should be an adverb: "However long the task takes, it will be done." For more on *however*, see pp. 144–145.

Hung. See *Hanged.*

The idea that. Like *the fact that*—and the cure is the same. Cut it.

If, whether. *If* is for uncertainties; *whether*, for alternatives. Usually the distinction is unimportant: *I don't know if it will rain; I don't know whether it will rain* [*or not*].

Imminent, Immanent. See *Eminent.*

Imply, infer. The author *implies;* you *infer* ("carry in") what you think he means.

He *implied* that all women are hypocrites.
From the ending, we *infer* that tragedy ennobles as it kills.

Importantly. Often an inaccurate (and popular) adverb, like *hopefully*.

INACCURATE	IMPROVED
More importantly, he walked home.	More important, he walked home.

In connection with. Always wordy. Say *about*.

POOR	IMPROVED
They liked everything in connection with the university.	They liked everything about the university.

Includes. Jargonish, as a general verb for specific actions.

POOR	IMPROVED
The report includes rural and urban marketing.	The report analyzes rural and urban marketing.

Individual. Write *person* unless you really mean someone separate and unique.

Infer. See *Imply, infer*.

Ingenious, ingenuous. Sometimes confused. *Ingenious* means clever; *ingenuous*, naïve. *Ingenius* is a common misspelling for both.

Instances. Redundant. *In many instances* means *often, frequently*.

Interesting. Make what you say interesting, but never tell the reader *it is interesting:* he may not believe you. *It is interesting* is merely a lazy preamble.

POOR	IMPROVED
It is interesting to note that nicotine is named for Jean Nicot, who introduced tobacco into France in 1560.	Nicotine is named for Jean Nicot, who introduced tobacco into France in 1560.

Irregardless. A faulty word. The *ir-* (meaning *not*) is doing what the *-less* already does. You are thinking of *irrespective*, and trying to say *regardless*.

Irregular Verbs. Here are some to watch; learn to control their past and past-participial forms. (See, also, *Hanged, hung; Lay; Rise, raise; Set, sit.*) Alternate forms are in parentheses.

arise, arose, arisen
awake, awoke, awaked (*but* was
    awakened)
bear, bore, borne

beat, beat, beaten
begin, began, begun
bid ("order"), bade, bidden
bid ("offer"), bid, bid

burst, burst, burst

drag, dragged (not drug), dragged

fit, fitted (fit, *especially intransitively*), fitted (*but* a fit person)

fling, flung, flung

get, got, got (gotten)

light, lit (lighted), lit (lighted)

prove, proved, proven (proved)

ride, rode, ridden

sew, sewed, sewn (sewed)

shine ("glow"), shone, shone

shine ("polish"), shined, shined

show, showed, shown (showed)

shrink, shrank (shrunk), shrunk (shrunken)

sow, sowed, sown (sowed)

spring, sprang, sprung

swim, swam, swum

swing, swung, swung

wake, woke (waked), waked

Is when, is where. Avoid these loose attempts:

LOOSE	SPECIFIC
Combustion is when [where] oxidation bursts into flame.	Combustion is oxidation bursting into flame.

It. Give it a specific reference, as a pronoun. See pp. 64, 131, 132.

Its, it's. Don't confuse *its,* the possessive pronoun, with *it's,* the contraction of *it is.*

-ize. A handy way to make verbs from nouns and adjectives *(patron-ize, civil-ize).* But handle with care. Manufacture new *-izes* only with a sense of humor and daring ("they Harvardized the party"). Business overdoes the trick: *finalize,* a relative newcomer, has provoked strong disapproval from writers who are not commercially familiarized.

Jargon. A technical, wordy phraseology that becomes characteristic of any particular trade, or branch of learning, frequently with nouns modifying nouns, and in the passive voice. Break out of it by making words mean what they say.

JARGON	CLEAR MEANING
The plot structure of the play provides no objective correlative.	The play fails to act out and exhibit the hero's inner conflicts.
	The plot is incoherent.
	The structure is lopsided.
The character development of the heroine is excellent.	The author sketches and deepens the heroine's personality skillfully.
	The heroine matures convincingly.
Three motivation profile studies were developed in the area of production management.	The company studied its production managers, and discovered three kinds of motivation.

Kind of, sort of. Colloquialisms for *somewhat, rather, something,* and the like. Usable, but don't overuse.

Lay. Don't use *lay* to mean *lie. To lay* means "to put" and needs an object; *to lie* means "to recline." Memorize both their present and past tenses, which are frequently confused:

> I *lie* down when I can; I *lay* down yesterday; I have *lain* down often. [Intransitive, no object.]
> The hen *lays* an egg; she *laid* one yesterday; she has *laid* four this week. [Transitive, *lays* an object.]
> Now I *lay* the book on the table; I *laid* it there yesterday; I have *laid* it there many times.

Lend, loan. Don't use *loan* for *lend. Lend* is the verb; *loan,* the noun: "Please *lend* me a five; I need a *loan* badly." Remember the line: "I'll *send* you to a *friend* who'll be willing to *lend.*"

Less, few. Don't use one for the other. *Less* answers "How much?" *Few* answers "How many?"

WRONG	RIGHT
We had *less* people than last time.	We had *fewer* people this time than last.

Level. Usually redundant jargon. *High-level management* is *top management* and *college-level courses* are *college courses.*

Lie, lay. See *Lay.*

Lighted, lit. Equally good past tenses for *light* (both "to ignite" and "to descend upon"), with *lit* perhaps more frequent. Rhythm usually determines the choice. *Lighted* seems preferred for adverbs and combinations: *a clean well-lighted place; it could have been lighted better.*

Like, as, as if. Usage blurs them, but the writer should distinguish them before he decides to go colloquial. Otherwise, he may throw his readers off.

> He looks *like* me.
> He dresses *as* [the way] I do.
> He acts *as if* he were high.

Note that *like* takes the objective case, and that *as,* being a conjunction, is followed by the nominative:

> She looks like *her.*
> He is as tall as *I* [am].
> He is tall, like *me.*

Like sometimes replaces *as* where no verb follows in phrases other than comparisons *(as . . . as):*

It works *like* **a charm. (**. . . *as* **a charm** *works*.**)**
It went over *like* **a lead balloon. (**. . . *as* **a lead balloon** *does*.**)**
They worked *like* **beavers. (**. . . *as* **beavers** *do*.**)**

Literally. Often misused, and overused, as a general emphasizer: "We *literally* wiped them off the field." Since the word means "by the letter," a *literal* meaning is distinct from a *figurative* meaning. *His heart was stone* means, literally, that his blood pump was, somehow, made of stone; it means, figuratively, "He was cruel." Avoid it unless you mean to show exactly what a word, or a statement, means: *To decapitate means literally to take the head off.*

Loan. See *Lend.*

Loose, lose. You will *lose* the game if your defense is *loose.*

Lots, lots of, a lot of. Conversational for *many, much, great, considerable.* Try something else. See *Alot.*

Maximum (minimum) amount. Drop *amount.* The minimum and the maximum *are* amounts. Don't write *a minimum of* and *as a minimum:* write *at least.*

May. See *Can, may.*

Maybe. Conversational for *perhaps.* Sometimes misused for *may be.* Unless you want an unmistakable colloquial touch, avoid it altogether.

Me. Use *me* boldly. It is the proper object of verbs and prepositions. Nothing is sadder than faulty propriety: "between you and *I*," or "They gave it to John and *I*," or "They invited my wife and *I*." Test yourself by dropping the first member: "between I" *(no)*, "gave it to I" *(no)*, "invited I" *(no)*. And do NOT substitute *myself.*

Medium, media. The singular and the plural. Avoid *medias,* unless you chose to begin *In medias res.*

Might. See *Can, may.*

Most. Does not mean *almost.*

WRONG	RIGHT
Most everyone knows.	Almost everyone knows.

Must, a must. *A must* is popular jargon. Try something else.

JARGON	IMPROVED
Beatup is really a *must* for every viewer.	Everyone interested in film should see *Beatup*.
This is a *must* course.	Everyone should take this course.

Myself. Use it only reflexively ("I hurt *myself*"), or intensively ("I *myself* often have trouble"). Fear of *me* leads to the incorrect "They gave it to John and *myself*." Do not use *myself, himself, herself, themselves* for *me, him, her, them*.

Nature. Avoid this padding. Do not write *moderate in nature, moderate by nature, of a moderate nature;* simply write *moderate*.

Near. Avoid using it for degree:

POOR	IMPROVED
a near perfect orbit	a nearly perfect orbit
	an almost perfect orbit
It was a near disaster.	It was nearly a disaster [*or* nearly disastrous].

Neither. See *Either*.

None. This pronoun means "no one" and takes a singular verb, as do *each, every, everyone, nobody*, and other distributives. See p. 126.

Nowhere near. Use *not nearly*, or *far from*, unless you really mean *near*: "He was nowhere near the end." See *Near*.

Number of. Usually correct. See *Amount of*.

Numbers. Spell out those that take no more than two words (*twelve, twelfth, twenty-four, two hundred);* use numerals for the rest (*101, 203, 4,510*). Spell out *all* numbers beginning a sentence. But use numerals to make contrasts and statistics clearer: *20 as compared to 49; only 1 out of 40; 200 or 300 times as great*. Change a two-word number to numerals when it matches a numeral: *with 400* [not *four hundred*] *students and 527 parents*. Numbers are customary with streets: *42nd Street, 5th Avenue*, which may also be spelled out for aesthetic reasons: *Fifth Avenue*. Use numbers also with dates, times, measurements, and money: *April 1, 1984; 6:30* A.M. (but *half-past six); 3 x 5 cards; 240 by 100 feet; 6'3"* (but *six feet tall); $4.99; $2 a ticket* (but *16 cents a bunch*).

Use Roman numerals together with Arabic to designate Act,

scene, and line in plays, and Book, chapter, and page in the novels that use them:

Romeo lies on the floor and cries like a child (III.iii.69–90).
When Tom Jones finds the banknote (XII.iv.483), ...

You would have already identified, in a footnote, the edition you are using. For further details see pp. 98–99; 101.

Off of. Write *from:* "He jumped *from* his horse."

On the part of. Wordy.

POOR	IMPROVED
There was a great deal of discontent *on the part of* those students who could not enroll.	The students who could not enroll were deeply discontented.

One. Avoid this common redundancy.

POOR	IMPROVED
One of the most effective ways of writing is rewriting.	The best writing is rewriting.
The Ambassadors is one of the most interesting of James's books.	*The Ambassadors* is James at his best.
The meeting was obviously a poor one.	The meeting was obviously poor.

In constructions such as "one of the best that . . ." and "one of the worst who . . . ," the relative pronouns often are mistakenly considered singular. The plural noun of the prepositional phrase *(the best, worst),* not *the one,* is the antecedent, and the verb must be plural too:

WRONG	RIGHT
one of the best [*players*] who *has* ever swung a bat	one of the best [*players*] who *have* ever swung a bat

Only. Don't put it in too soon; you will say what you do not mean.

WRONG	RIGHT
He *only liked* mystery stories.	He liked *only* mystery stories.

Overall. Jargonish. Use *general,* or rephrase.

DULL	IMPROVED
The overall quality was good.	The lectures were generally good.

Per. Use *a:* "He worked ten hours *a* day." *Per* is jargonish, except in conventional Latin phrases: *per diem, per capita* (not italicized in your running prose).

POOR	IMPROVED
This will cost us a manhour *per* machine *per* month a year from now.	A year from now, this will cost us a manhour a machine a month.
As *per* your instructions	According to your instructions

Per cent, percent, percentage. *Percent* (one word) seems preferred, though *percentage,* without numbers, still carries polish: "A large *percentage* of nonvoters attended"; "a significant *percentage* of the students." Use the % sign and numerals only when comparing percentages, and in technical reports. Otherwise spell out "percent" with the numbers: *ten percent, a hundred percent* (see *Numbers*).

Perfect. Not "more perfect," but "more nearly perfect."

Personally. Almost always superfluous.

POOR	IMPROVED
I want to welcome them *personally.*	I want to welcome them [myself].
Personally, I like it.	I like it.

Phase. Do not use when *part* is wanted; "a *phase* of the organization" is better put as "a *part* of the organization." A phase is a stage in a cycle, as of the moon, of business, of the financial markets, and so on.

Phenomena. Frequently misused for the singular *phenomenon:* "This is a striking *phenomenon*" (not *phenomena*).

Phenomenal. Misused for a general intensive: "His popularity was *phenomenal.*" A phenomenon is a fact of nature, in the ordinary nature of things. Find another word for the extraordinary: "His success was *extraordinary*" (*unusual, astounding, stupendous*).

Plan on. Use *plan to.* "He planned on going" should be "He planned to go."

Prejudice. When you write "He was *prejudice,*" your readers may be *puzzle.* Give it a *d:* "He was *prejudiced*"; then they won't be *puzzled.*

Presently. Drop it. Or use *now.* Many readers will take it to mean *soon:* "He will go *presently.*" It is characteristic of official jargon.

POOR	IMPROVED
The committee is meeting *presently*.	The committee is meeting.
	The committee is meeting *soon*.
He is *presently* studying Greek.	He is studying Greek.

Principle, principal. Often confused. *Principle* is a noun only, meaning an essential truth, or rule: "It works on the *principle* that hot air rises." Princi*pal* is the *a*djective: The high-school *principal* acts as a noun because usage has dropped the *person* the adjective once modified. Likewise, *principal* is the principal amount of your money, which draws interest.

Process. Often verbal fat. For example, the following can reduce more often than not: *production process,* to *production; legislative* (or *legislation*) *process,* to *legislation; educational* (or *education*) *process,* to *education; societal process* to *social forces.*

Proof, evidence. *Proof* results from enough *evidence* to establish a point beyond doubt. Be modest about claiming proof:

POOR	IMPROVED
This *proves* that Fielding was in Bath at the time.	Evidently, Fielding was in Bath at the time.

Provide. If you *absolutely cannot* use the meaningful verb directly, you may say *provide,* provided you absolutely cannot *give, furnish, allow, supply, enable, authorize, permit, facilitate, force, do, make, effect, help, be, direct, cause, encourage . . . .*

Providing that. Use *provided,* and drop the *that. Providing,* with or without *that,* tends to make a misleading modification.

POOR	IMPROVED
I will drop, *providing that* I get an incomplete.	I will drop, *provided* I get an incomplete.

In "I will drop, *providing that* I get an incomplete," *you* seem to be providing, contrary to what you mean.

Put across. Try something else: *convinced, persuaded, explained, made clear. Put across* is badly overused.

Quality. Keep it as a noun. Too many *professional quality writers* are already producing *poor quality prose,* and *poor in quality* means *poor.*

Quite. An acceptable but overused emphatic: *quite good, quite expressive, quite a while, quite a person.* Try rephrasing it now and then: *good, very good, for some time, an able person.*

Quote, quotation. Quote your quotations, and put them in quotation marks. Distinguish the verb from the noun. The best solution is to use *quote* only as a verb and to find synonyms for the noun: *passage, remark, assertion.*

WRONG	RIGHT
As the following quote from Milton shows:	As the following passage [or quotation] from Milton shows: . . . .

Raise. See *Rise, raise.*

Rarely ever. Drop the *ever:* "Shakespeare *rarely* misses a chance for comedy."

Real. Do not use for *very. Real* is an adjective meaning "actual":

WRONG	RIGHT
It was *real* good.	It was *very* good.
	It was *really* good.

Reason . . . is because. Knock out *the reason . . . is,* and *the reason why . . . is,* and you will have a good sentence.

[The reason] they have difficulty with languages [is] because they have no interest in them.

Regarding, in regard to. Redundant or inaccurate.

POOR	IMPROVED
Regarding the banknote, Jones was perplexed. [Was he *looking* at it?]	Jones was perplexed by the banknote.
He knew nothing *regarding* money.	He knew nothing about money.
She was careful *in regard to* the facts.	She respected the facts.

Regardless. This is correct. See *Irregardless* for the confusion.

Respective, respectively. Usually redundant.

POOR	IMPROVED
The armies retreated to their *respective* trenches.	The armies retreated to their trenches.
Smith and Jones won the first and second prize *respectively.*	Smith won the first prize; Jones, the second.

Reverend, Honorable. Titles of clergymen and congressmen. The fully proper forms, as in the heading of a letter (*the* would not be capitalized in your running prose), are *The Reverend Mr. Claude C. Smith; The Honorable Adam A. Jones.* In running prose,

Rev. Claude Smith and *Hon. Adam Jones* will get by, but the best procedure is to give the title and name its full form for first mention, then to continue with *Mr. Smith* and *Mr. Jones.* Do not use "Reverend" or "Honorable" with the last name alone.

Rise, raise. Frequently confused. *Rise, rose, risen* means to get up. *Raise, raised, raised* means to lift up. "He *rose* early and *raised* a commotion."

Sanction. Beatifically ambiguous, now meaning both "to approve" and "to penalize." Stick to the root; use it only "to bless," "to sanctify," "to approve," "to permit." Use *penalize* or *prohibit* when you mean just that. Instead of "They exacted *sanctions*," say "They exacted *penalties*."

Seldom ever. Redundant. Cut the *ever.* (But *seldom if ever* has its uses.)

Set, sit. Frequently confused. You *set* something down; you yourself *sit* down. Confine sitting to people (*sit, sat, sat*), and keep it intransitive, taking no object. *Set* is the same in all tenses (*set, set, set*).

CONFUSED	CLARIFIED
The house *sets* too near the street.	The house *stands* (*is*) too near the street.
The package *sat* where he left it.	The package *lay* where he left it.
He *has set* there all day.	He *has sat* there all day.

Shall, will; should, would. The older distinctions—*shall* and *should* reserved for *I* and *we*—have faded; *will* and *would* are usual: "I will go"; "I would if I could"; "he will try"; "they all would." *Shall* in the third person expresses determination: "They shall not pass." *Should,* in formal usage, is actually ambiguous: *We should be happy to comply,* intended to mean "would be happy," seems to say "ought to be happy."

Should of. See *Could of, would of.*

Similar to. Use *like:*

POOR	IMPROVED
This is *similar to* that.	This is *like* that.

Sit. See *Set, sit.*

Situate. Usually wordy and inaccurate. Avoid it unless you mean, literally or figuratively, the act of determining a site, or placing a building: "Do not *situate* heavy buildings on loose soil."

FAULTY	IMPROVED
Ann Arbor is a town *situated* on the Huron River.	Ann Arbor is a town on the Huron River.
The control panel is *situated* on the right.	The control panel is on the right.
He is well *situated*.	He is rich.
The company is well *situated* to meet the competition.	The company is well prepared to meet the competition.

Situation. Usually jargon. Avoid it. Say what you mean: *state, market, mess, quandary, conflict, predicament.*

Size. Often redundant. *A small-sized country* is *a small country. Large in size* is *large.*

Slow. GO SLOW is what the street signs and the people on the street all say, but write "Go slowly."

So. Should be followed by *that* in describing extent: "It was *so* foggy *that* traffic almost stopped." Avoid its incomplete form, the teen-ager's intensive—*so nice, so wonderful, so pretty*—though occasionally this is effective.

Someplace, somewhere. See *Anyplace.*

Sort of. See *Kind of, sort of.*

Split infinitives. Improve them. They are cliché traps: *to really know, to really like, to better understand.* They are one of the signs of a wordy writer, and usually produce redundancies: *to really understand* is *to understand.* The quickest cure for split infinitives is to drop the adverb.

For a gain in grace, and often for a saving of words, you can sometimes change the adverb to an adjective:

POOR	IMPROVED
to **adequately** *think* **out solutions**	*to think* **out adequate solutions**
to enable us *to* **effectively** *plan* **our advertising**	**to enable us** *to plan* **effective advertising**

Structure. A darling of the jargoneer, often meaning nothing more framelike than "unity" or "coherence." *Plot structure* usually means *plot*, with little idea of beams and girders. Use it only for something you could diagram, like the ribs of a snake, and never use it as a verb. See *Jargon.*

POOR	IMPROVED
He structured the meeting.	He organized (planned, arranged) the meeting.

Sure. Too colloquial for writing: "It is *sure* a good plan." Use *surely* or *certainly,* or rephrase.

Tautology. Several words serving where fewer—usually one—are needed, or wanted: useless repetition. Some examples:

attach [together]	mix [together]
[basic] essentials	[pair of] twins
consecutive days [in a row]	(but, two *sets* of twins)
[early] beginnings	[past] history
[final] completion	refer [back]
[final] upshot	repeat [again]
[first] beginnings	sufficient [enough]
[just] merely	whether [or not]

That, which, who. *That* defines and restricts; *which* is explanatory and nonrestrictive; *who* stands for people, and may be restrictive or nonrestrictive. See pp. 46, 48, 64–66.

There is, there are, it is. However natural and convenient—it is WORDY. Notice that *it* here refers to something specific, differing distinctly from the *it* in "It is easy to write badly." (Better: "Writing badly is easy.") This indefinite subject, like *there is* and *there are,* gives the trouble. Of course, you will occasionally need an *it* or a *there* to assert existences:

There are ants in the cupboard.	There are craters on the moon.
There is only one Kenneth.	It is too bad.

They. Often a loose indefinite pronoun; tighten it. See pp. 131, 132.

Till, until. Both are respectable. Note the spelling. Do not use *'til.*

Too. Awful as a conjunctive adverb: "Too, it was unjust." Also poor as an intensive: "They did not do too well" (note the difference in Shakespeare's "not wisely but too well"—he really means it). Use *very,* or (better) nothing: "They did not do well" (notice the nice understated irony).

Tool. Overused for "means." Try *instrument, means.*

Toward, towards. *Toward* is the better (towards in Britain), though both are acceptable.

Trite. From Latin *tritus:* "worn out." Many words get temporarily worn out and unusable: *emasculated, viable, situation,* to name a few. And many phrases are permanently frayed; see *Clichés.*

Type. Banish it, abolish it. If you must use it, insert *of:* not *that type person* but *that type OF person,* though even this is really jargon for *that kind of person, a person like that.* See p. 67.

Unique. Something *unique* has nothing in the world like it.

WRONG	RIGHT
The more unique the organiza- tion	The more nearly unique . . . .
the most unique man I know	the most unusual man I know
a very unique personality	a unique personality

Use, use of. A dangerously wordy word. See p. 66.

Use to. A mistake for *used to.*

Utilize, utilization. Like *use,* wordy. See p. 66.

POOR	IMPROVED
He *utilizes* frequent dialogue to enliven his stories.	Frequent dialogue enlivens his stories.
The *utilization* of a scapegoat eases their guilt.	A scapegoat eases their guilt.

Very. Spare the *very* and the *quite, rather, pretty,* and *little.* I would hate to admit (and don't care to know) how many of these qualifiers I have cut from this text. You can do without them entirely, but they do ease a phrase now and then.

Viable. With *feasible,* overworked. Try *practicable, workable, possible.*

Ways. Avoid it for distance. Means *way:* "He went a short *way* into the woods."

Well. See *Good.*

Whether. See *If.*

Which. See *Who, which, that.*

While. Reserve for time only, as in "*While* I was talking, she smoked constantly." Do not use for *although.*

WRONG	RIGHT
While I like her, I don't admire her.	*Although* I like her, I don't admire her.

Who, which, that. *Who* may be either restrictive or nonrestrictive: "The ones *who win* are lucky"; "The players, *who are all out-*

standing, win often." *Who* refers only to persons. Use *that* for all other restrictives; *which* for all other nonrestrictives. Cut every *who, that,* and *which* not needed. See pp. 64–65, "the *of-and-which* disease" (pp. 64–66), and, on restrictives, and non-restrictives, p. 65.

Avoid *which* in loose references to the whole idea preceding, rather than to a specific word, since you may be unclear:

FAULTY	IMPROVED
He never wore the hat, which his wife hated.	His wife hated his going bare-headed.
	He never wore the hat his wife hated.

Whom, whomever. The objective forms, after verbs and prepositions; but each is often wrongly put as the subject of a clause (p. 130).

WRONG	RIGHT
Give the ticket to *whomever* wants it.	Give the ticket to *whoever wants it.* [The whole clause is the object of *to; whoever* is the subject of *wants.*]
The president, *whom* he said would be late	The president, *who* he said *would be late* . . . . [Commas around *he said* would clear the confusion.]
Whom shall I say called?	*Who* shall I say called?

BUT:
They did not know *whom* to elect. [The infinitive takes the objective case.]

Who's, whose. Sometimes confused in writing. *Who's* means "who is?" in conversational questions: *"Who's* going?" Never use it in writing (except in dialogue), and you can't miss. *Whose* is the regular possessive of *who:* "The committee, *whose* work was finished, adjourned."

Will. See *Shall.*

-wise. Avoid all confections like *marketwise, customerwise, pricewise, gradewise, confectionwise* — except for humor.

Would. For habitual acts, the simple past is more economical:

POOR	IMPROVED
The parliament *would meet* only when called by the king.	The parliament *met* only when called by the king.
Every hour, the watchman *would make* his round.	Every hour, the watchman *made* his round.

Would sometimes seeps into the premise of a supposition. Rule: Don't use *would* in an *if* clause.

WRONG	RIGHT
If he *would have* gone, he would have succeeded.	If he *had* gone, he would have succeeded.
	Had he gone, he would have succeeded [more economical].

Would of. See *Could of, would of.*

EXERCISES

Refer to the Glossary and your dictionary as needed to clear up the following passages.

1. The US is presently leading the debate in the UN, *viz.* that concerning the energy crisis problem, accept for atomic research. They hope to reach an accomodation that will not effect the general economy or endanger the enviorment. Every country has their own point of view, of course, answers are not easily forthcoming and many smaller powers are disallusioned by the dilemna, since delay may be disasterous, due to the fact that all countries face inflation. Some countries could care less. Some enthuse over prospects of high level profits from their principle exports, proceding to further fan the flames of arguement and resistence. An explosion is immanent.

2. Some students are prejudice unconsciously, and would never apollogize, no matter what occured. They are frequently not as considerate as those that appreciate the minoritys' point of view. They would have acted more maturely, if they would have been more socially aware, as of the 20th century. But everyday less students make these errors. Some courses in the regular curicula are a definate must for social awareness, since they cause the ballance of the students to discover their hidden prejudice, in may cases. These kind of courses center around the concept of how prejudice is acquired, and cause the student to understand his attitudes in connection with society.

3. Originality is a rare-type phenomena. Each creation may seem discreet to its creator, however, it usually resembles many others of it's type, even works of reknowned authors. These kind of works are actually enjoyable because we see the resemblances together with the differences. None of the performances of the same symphony are the same for each rewards anew. We persue novelty without realizing that we want similiarity too. The particular performance

disolves into our general memory of the familiar work. The reason why we can listen to the same symphony, or see the same play, or even the same film again and again is because each experience is seperate and new. In the field of aesthetics, the performance gives us satisfaction if it has fit our general memory of the work. A memory that also changes slightly with each performance, resulting in a more perfect idea of the work, untill our idea takes on a kind of permanent existance.

4. Swimming is healthy, a never to be forgotten experience, it is believed by some authorities that it is the most generally healthy exercise transpiring. Many just lay on the beach and soak in the sun but it is sheer hypocracy as well as being lazy. In fact, many students like to infer that they have gone to Florida while they only have been sunning under a lamp in his/her room. Some sunning is alright, of course but too much will result in a burn and a poor quality tan. People using caution rarely ever get burned, especially with the use of an unchallangable lotion.

Index

a, an, 163*
abbreviations, 100–102, 163–164; alphabetizing of, 89–90; of page numbers, 97; of titles, 98, 101
ablative absolute, 51–52
absolute phrases, 51–52
abstraction, 73–74
active voice, 45, 62–65, 68, 129
adapt, adopt, 164
adjectival clause, defined, 124
adjectival phrase, defined, 124
adjectives, 124, 132–134; hyphenated, 154; nouns as, 66–67, 68; parallel, 52, 53; participles as, 65, 124–125; pronouns as, 123; in series, 146
adjectives-with-phrase construction, 50
adverbial clause, defined, 124
adverbial phrase, defined, 124
adverbs, 132–134, 135; defined, 124; hyphenated, 154
after, 46, 48
affect, effect, 165
agreement of subject and verb, 125–127; in subjunctive, 128–129
alliteration, 74
all right, alright, 165
allusion, 77–78, 165
alot, 165
alphabetizing: bibliography, 96, 102–103, 104; in card catalogs, 87–90; encyclopedias and, 98
although, 46, 48–49
an, a, 163
analogy, false, 41
and, 45, 46, 53, 80; comma with, 141, 142, 145
and/or, 155, 165
Anglo-Saxon words, 71–72, 78–79; spelling, 157
anonymous works, 103, 104

antecedents of pronouns, 131–132; defined, 123, 129
any, 166
anyone, 126
appositives, 49–50; double, 146
apostrophe, 153–154
argument: description in, 28–30, 33–34; evidence in, 37–41, 86, 93–94, 183; progression of, 8–12; progression diagrams, 12, 13–14, 25; research thesis and, 92, 93–95; thesis selection and, 2–6, 86
argumentative edge, 2–4
Aristotle: cited, 8, 146, 162; quoted, 44, 78, 80
articles (grammar), 124, 163
as, 130, 166; compared with *like,* 178–179
as if, 48, 167, 178–179
assumptions, examination of, 4, 5, 6, 38, 41
as well as, parallel construction, 53, 167
asyndeton, 146
atlases, 87
Austen, Jane, 77
authorities, citation of, 39–40, 92; research and, 86, 87, 95–103

Bacon, Francis, quoted, 55
Baldwin, James, quoted, 21–22
because, 46, 48, 184; compared with *due to,* 172
begging the question, as logical fallacy, 5, 41
between, among, 168
Bible, The, 101, 152
bibliography, 85, 87, 90; compilation of, 91–93, 102–103, 104; sample, 120
Biography Index, 91
Bittner, William, quoted, 77
Book of Common Prayer, quoted, 49

* Refer to the Glossary of Usage, p. 163 ff., for words, prefixes, suffixes, and phrases not listed in the Index.

192

Book Review Digest, 91
both/and, 53
brackets, 149; in footnotes, 99; with sic, 100
British usage, variations in, 126, 150
but, 20, 45, 46, 54, 168; in argument, 12; commas and, 141, 142, 144–145
by, 61, 80

Camus, Albert, 77
can, may, 168–169
cannot but, 168
capitalization, 158–160, 169; of Biblical references, 101; in bibliography, 102; in dates, 164; hyphens and, 154
cards: bibliographical, 91–93, 102–103, 104; library catalog, 87–90
Carmichael, Stokely, quoted, 38–39
case, 169
case (pronouns), 123
catalogs, library, 87–90, 92
Catullus, 162–163
cause and effect, 68
cf. (confer), 100
Chamber's Encyclopaedia, 87
Cicero, 162–163
clarity, 61–68, 163; redundancy and, 79–82; vocabulary and, 71–73, 78–79
clauses, 10–11, 46, 125; adverbial, 124; modifying, 49–50; non-restrictive, 142–145, 148; noun clauses, 122–123; restrictive, 50, 65; subject-verb structure of, 48
clichés, 61, 66–67; dead metaphors in, 76–77, 170
coherence: of paragraphs, 17–18, 31–32; of essays, 24–26
collective nouns: defined, 122–123; agreement and, 126, 127
Collier's Encyclopedia, 87
:olon, 46, 47, 147–148; capitalization after, 159; quotation marks and, 150
Columbia Encyclopedia, 87
comma, 12, 99, 140–146; in Biblical references, 101; in compound sentences, 46–47; compression and, 147; dashes and, 148; parentheses and, 96, 97; with quotation marks, 98, 150
comma splice, 135
common nouns, defined, 122–123
comparisons, 12; false analogies, 41; completion of, 133; see also metaphor
Compleat Angler, The (Walton), 33
complex sentences: defined, 45–46; parallel constructions in, 52–56; subordination in, 47–49
compound sentences: defined, 45–46; punctuation of, 46–47

conjunctions, 45–46, 47; defined, 125; see also specific conjunctions
conjunctive adverbs, 46–47, 135
connectives, 46, 48, 55
consequently, 46–47
consonants: a before, 163; in spelling 155–156
contractions, 171
contrast, rhetorical, 12; semicolons and, 47, 147
coordinating conjunctions, 46–47, 53–54, 125; commas and, 141, 142
coordinator comma, 141–142; defined, 140
could care less, 171
could of, would of, 171
Cowley, Malcolm, quoted, 76
Current Biography Index, 91
curriculums, 171

Dahlberg, Edward, quoted, 79
dangling participles, 51
dangling infinitives, 134
dash, 55, 148–149
definition process, 38–39, 80–81
demonstrative pronouns, defined, 123
description, 28–30
detail, 28–30; in narrative, 31
DeVries, Peter, quoted, 78
diacritical marks, 157
dialectic order, 10–12, 24
diction, 78–82; wordiness, 79–81; overcultivation of, 81–82
dictionaries, 72–73, 154; spelling and, 155, 157–158, 160
double apposition, 146
double negative, 172
double possessive, 154
Dryden, John, 74
due to, 172

each, 126
Eddington, Sir Arthur, quoted, 39–40
editors, 100; bibliographic citation of, 103
Einstein, Albert, 39–40
either/or, logical fallacy of, 41
either/or parallel construction, 53, 54; agreement and, 126–127
Eliot, T. S., 99; quoted, 73, 163
ellipsis, 152–153
emphasis, 45, 140; capitalization and, 159; commas and, 146; hyphens and, 154; quotations and, 95; subordination and, 47–49
Encyclopaedia Britannica, 87
Encyclopedia Americana, 87
enthuse, 173
Essay and General Literature Index, 91

so, 22, 45, 47, 186; comma and, 47, 142
Social Sciences Index, 91
so that, 48
speech, parts of, 122–125
spelling, 155–158; foreign words, 158; numbers, 180; troublesome words (list), 158
split infinitives, 186
squinting modifiers, 133–134
statistics, as evidence, 40–41
Stewart, Randall, quoted, 92
still, 47; comma and, 142
structure, 8–14; ascending interest, 9–10; comparison and contrast, 12; of essays, 24–26; *pro-con* alteration, 10–14
style, 1–2, 73; Aristotle on, 78, 80; Cowley on Hawthorne's, 76; Ransom on, 79
subject, 44, 45; of clause 48; comma placement and, 140–141; fragments and, 134–135; of infinitives, 125, 130; in passive voice, 62, 63; pronouns as, 130; verb, agreement of, 125–127
subjective pronouns, *see* nominative pronouns
subjunctive mood, 128–129
subordinate clauses, 10, 46, 48, 139–140; ablative absolute in, 51–52; as appositives, 49–50; parallel construction and, 53–55, 56; participles in, 50–51; subjunctive mood in, 128–129
subordinating conjunction, defined, 125
subordination: in complex sentences, 46, 47–49; modification and, 49–51; phrases and, 139
such as, 166
suffixes, 155
summation, 8, 22–23; punctuation and, 55
sure, 187
syllables in words, hypenation of, 154–155
synonyms, 73, 78

tautology, 187
tense of verb, 127–128; shifts, 32
than, 130
that, 46, 48–49, 64, 68; in parallel constructions, 55; referent-verb agreement, 129; *which* and, 65, 187, 188–189
that was, 65
then, 22, comma and, 142; semicolon and, 147
their, they're, 153
therefore, 20, 46–47, 135, 147
thesaurus, 73
thesis, 2–6, 8, 18; dialectic demonstration of, 10–14; illustrative evidence for, 37–41, 93–94; paragraph structure and, 18–

20, 22–23, 24, 25; in research paper, 86–87, 92, 93, 95
they, as indefinite pronoun, 132
this, 131
Thoreau, Henry David, quoted, 76, 77–78
thus, 22
Times Atlas of the World, The, 87
title page, research paper, 104
titles: alphabetizing in bibliographies, 102, 104; capitalization of, 159; footnote treatment of, 97–99, 101–102; italics and, 151–152
to be, 64
too, 187
topic sentences, 17–18, 19, 25; transitions and, 20–21, 22
transitional devices, 20–22
transitional phrases, 135
transitive verb, 132; defined, 123
triteness, 3, 19, 188; *see also* clichés
type, 67, 188
typing, 104; bibliography, 102–103; brackets, 149; dashes, 149; footnotes, 96, 101–102; italics, 151; quotations, 95–96

United States Library of Congress, 88
unity, *see* coherence
unique, 188
until, 48
usage, 163–190; British, 126, 150; dictionaries and, 87, 160; fashions in, 162–163; italics and, 151, 152
use, 65–66, 188
utilize, utilization, 65–66, 188

verbosity, *see* wordiness
verbs, 122, 123; in clause structure, 48; comma placement and, 140, 142; implied, 130; implied metaphor in, 76; irregular, listed, 176–177; mood alignment, 128–129; parallel, 53, 55; participles and, 124–125; in periodic sentences, 44, 45; principle parts, 176; subject, agreement with, 125–127; tense alignment, 128–129; voice, 45, 51, 62–65, 68, 127, 129
viewpoint, 3; confidence in, 6–7; definition and, 38–39; exposition and, 33–34; intrusive, 31–32; sharpening of, 4–6, 22–23; *see also* thesis
virgule, 150
vocabulary, 71–82
vowels, 156, 163

Walden (Thoreau), 77
Walton, Izaak, quoted, 33–34
way, ways, 188

77 78 79 80 81 7 6 5 4 3 2